THE MECHANICS OF MARRIAGE

Is Your Relationship Due for a Tune-Up?

D1521442

By: Drs. Jomo and Charmaine Cousins

TABLE OF CONTENTS

INTRODUCTION

Let's take a drive. The journey will be long. The ride will get bumpy, there will be many detours, and we will surely encounter some less than favorable elements along the way. The final destination, however, will be worth everything you face and will be more beautiful than you could ever imagine.

But before we ride off into the sunset, we should prepare for our trip ahead. What are some of the must-dos to ensure we have everything we need to reach our final destination?

A trustworthy, reliable vehicle? Check.

Fuel? Check.

A map or GPS? Check.

Two willing and enthusiastic drivers? Check.

Outside of some snacks and electronics, it looks like we have the basics covered. Time to buckle up and hit the road, right?

Well, there's just one catch. The journey we are about to embark on is marriage. And just like a preparing for a road trip, we must ask ourselves if we are truly ready for the journey ahead. Do we have the basic items needed to go the distance?

Love?

Communication?

Trust?

Respect?

God?

Will we lose momentum along the way due to lack of fuel, or one or both of us takes a detour? Will we have support if our vehicle breaks down? And finally, will we be able to roll up our sleeves and look under the hood as needed to ensure we can prevent and fix issues as they arise.

Marriage is for people who are enduring and persevering because the road to happiness is long.

Many couples end up separating because they struggle to wait for God to prune, shape, and transform them. Couples who celebrate several years of marriage and are stable and happy have just realized that they need to give themselves time to appreciate the grace of God that they have been given to be united.

The happiness that you hope for in marriage comes through perseverance. Like a car, our marriages all need tune-ups from time to time. There will be highs and lows, times to celebrate together and times to have those tough conversations. It's all what makes marriage what it is!

James 1:4 says, *"You must learn to endure everything, so you will be completely mature and not lacking in anything."* Every time we experience a trial together, we have one of two options: we either let it bring us closer together or pull us further apart. The more that we choose to grow together through the struggles we face in life, the more we mature both individually and as a couple. There is a path toward consistent and continual growth in marriage, and that's the path we're going to find together in this book.

So be patient in making your decisions to avoid the regrets, the conflict, and the heartbreak. Cherish the bond you have together and enjoy this beautiful gift you've been given. Commit right now to putting in the hard work because IT IS SO WORTH IT.

Marriage is a beautiful thing. Many today see it as broken, but marriage isn't broken; people break a marriage. How you foster growth together, treat one another, and communicate determines whether you succeed or fail. In marriage, God has gifted you with something incredible, and you have the power to make it thrive. It takes genuine devotion to see a marriage through to the fruition it truly deserves.

Many are suffering from marriages where they are drifting apart instead of growing closer together. Time, responsibilities, and the rigors of life set in, putting hurdles in the married couple's path.

I assure you that not only can you clear these hurdles, but you can often prevent them. On the other side, you will find a marriage that can go the distance. This reinvigorated love will draw you and your spouse closer than ever before, and you will experience God's design for a healthy marriage.

The mindset I am speaking of is, "marriage is just a piece of paper." Ever hear that one? There has been so much pain, and so many trials people have endured through conflict in marriage that it has cultivated this kind of attitude in us. I long to make a step towards instilling different feelings towards marriage in all of us, because God has shown me something immeasurably beautiful. It's something that I believe God desires for everyone who experiences marriage in this life to take part in.

In **Mark 10,** Jesus is teaching about marriage. He starts by saying, *"from the beginning of creation, 'God made them male and female.'"* This shows that God's original intent, from the very beginning of human history, was that His image would be reflected through humanity in both masculine and feminine aspects. The complexities of both sexes in their very own ways would reflect the image of God. They would come together, through relationship blessed by their creator, in order to fill the world with new life.

Here we find a foundational truth about humanity,

one that forms the very basis of all of our lives. Think about it: we all come from the same place. No matter how broken, how fragmented the relationship of our parents, two people come together in relationship brought us into this world. A lot of us have survived the crushing pain of being a child of divorce or coming from a broken relationship. For a lot of us, it has skewed our perception of marriage and stolen all of the value out of it in our eyes.

But we can't express this strongly enough: we need to look at it the completely opposite way. Just because people mess up marriage doesn't mean that marriage itself is the problem. Marriage isn't broken: people break marriage. We firmly believe one big reason for that is because we've completely forgotten, or maybe never knew in the first place, what it really is.

Marriage, and everything that we do within it, is an act of worship to God. Yes, spending time with your spouse is an act of worship to God. Having sex with your spouse is an act of worship to God. Raising your children is an act of worship to God. Striving to become one with your spouse in body and mind is an act of worship to God.

Marriage is a beautiful thing. God designed it from His boundless, creative mind and gave it to us as a gift that would enrich our lives. Through marriage, man and woman, both made in the image of God, come together in a special union that reflects the nature of God Himself. This results in an intimacy and companionship unlike any other relationship we could ever have. What could be better?

Yet, we live in a fallen world. Sin has reared its ugly head into our reality and sunk its claws deep into the foundation of our world. Its impact affects everything, even marriage. See, a marriage is made up of two people, each born inherently sinful. That makes marriage challenging, as two imperfect people strive to live as one and often clash.

So, marriage takes a lot of work. But does that make it not worth it? Should we then avoid marriage entirely? Absolutely not! Before we dive into the ins and outs of building the best marriage possible, we need to tell you this: every second of work you put into your marriage is worth it. Yes, there will be challenging times. Yes, there will be conflict. But if you do the work, you will get the reward: God's perfect design for the most beautiful human relationship you'll ever experience.

Even if you find marriage going smoothly, your relationship requires proper maintenance and service just like a vehicle. If you don't do regular check-ups how will you know when there is a problem or if a tune-up is due? Together, we are going to learn the Mechanics of Marriage and what you need to do to ensure your marriage is able to go the distance.

This book will be offered as a helpful guide to some of the normal challenges couples face and how to overcome those challenges with God at the center of the solutions provided. We wrote this book to help you along every step of your marriage journey. It doesn't matter if you are still dating, engaged, or already married: the wisdom in this book will prepare you for each evolution of your relationship. We will deal with real-life issues and address topics that many may not feel comfortable talking about that are integral to a relationship's success. Our hope is that after reading this book, you will have a better understanding of the mechanics of marriage and by applying these principles you will be able to cruise towards a loving, prosperous and fulfilling life with your spouse.

CHAPTER 1:

The Reality of Conflict

"When we learn to respond to each other rather than react, we will move much more quickly in our conflict toward resolution and reconciliation. Reactions only stoke the fires of conflict; responses, particularly godly ones, help us snuff out the conflict."

-Matt Chandler-

Ever hear that young, newlywed couple that vows never to argue with one another? It's a virtuous goal with the best of intentions, but let's be honest: that's pretty unrealistic!

We knew a couple who made the same promise in front of me. We tried to explain to them the things I'm about to share with you, but they were adamant that conflict was not going to EVER be a part of their marriage.

Fast-forward just a few months into their marriage, and Alan came to us distraught over a conflict that had developed and been left unresolved. It wasn't even a very big conflict (think neglecting to tell your spouse something kind of deal) but because the couple had not prepared to resolve conflict when it arises, they were left shell-shocked and hurt over something that never needed to last that long to begin with.

Instead of avoiding conflict whatsoever (which remember is not possible), we must learn how to navigate it and resolve it. This is one of the most essential skills that you can have as a couple. Your marriage depends on it!

The sad truth of the matter is that the statistics show that marriages are crumbling, even among Christians. The divorce rate has skyrocketed compared to years past. Seeing this sharp increase in numbers makes it evident that something is very wrong in our relationships. But what is it?

A large part of it is that we've simply forgotten how to resolve conflict. Things come up, as they always do in life. In any relationship in our fallen world, tension will arise, resulting in conflict that needs to be resolved. Why does this conflict need to be resolved? Because if it's not it will create feelings of anger, sadness, and resentment that will fester within our hearts. Those feelings will reside within us, growing until they rip through our lives like a whirlwind. That's why we must deal with the conflict as soon as possible after it arises.

Has your car ever made a strange noise while you were driving, and you tried your best to just explain it away or ignore it? Then it happens the next day, and the next, all while you try to push it out of your mind? Getting your car fixed can be a headache! It's expensive, you have to spend time without your vehicle, and you never know when a mechanic is trying to sell you a service you don't actually need.

But, if you don't get that sound checked out, it will get louder and louder. Whatever is going on with your car will get worse and worse until it's impossible to ignore. Then, resolving the situation will only be that much more challenging. Or, even worse, you might not be able to salvage your vehicle at all, no matter how much you try. It might be goodbye for good, all because you didn't take care of the issue when it arose.

Sadly, many people experience the same thing in marriage. Small conflicts left unresolved grow and fester within our hearts. They build and build, turning small things that could have been resolved easily into monsters of conflict completely out of our control. At that point, it takes an incredible amount of work to turn that marriage around. Most of the time, there will be lasting scars that will never go away. Even worse, many people have and continue to lose their entire marriage over this same scenario.

But it doesn't have to be this way! Having a healthy understanding of conflict resolution in marriage is all you need to ride the waves of conflict to the other side. And you know what's amazing about the whole process? Even though it's hard, it makes your marriage even STRONGER on the other side! Working through these things together in a loving and godly way promotes a unity and love like no other.

It's helpful to look at the conflict between you as an external force attacking your marriage. Instead of defending yourself against your spouse, you and your spouse are joining together against a common enemy. So often we combat our spouses trying to prove that we're right or innocent. But that's a destructive mindset that only leads to more conflict. Instead of trying to protect ourselves at all costs, we must fight with all our might to protect our marriage at all costs.

In the trenches together, you and your spouse will grow closer than ever before. Together, you will learn skills and strategies that will serve you for the rest of your lives. Marriage doesn't have to get harder as you get older. It CAN get stronger and easier, but you have to put in the work together of learning and practicing godly conflict resolution.

Conflict is part of every marriage. Couples bring their differences and expectations into the marriage, and inevitably there are fireworks. But when they learn how to navigate through conflict successfully, couples will find their relationship growing stronger.

Replacing Conflict with Peace

We need to rewire our thinking when it comes to how we approach conflict with our spouse. For many of us, our initial response is to come in combative and defensive. Whatever sparked the conflict in the first place can easily blind us. Instead of seeing our spouse as our partner and the person we love, we view them as the enemy. We must flee from this tendency at all costs. You are ONE with your spouse! When you fight against them instead of by their side, you are only starting a civil war with yourself!

Commit to always striving toward peace with your spouse. When you need to approach them with a touchy or challenging topic, come to them in love instead of anger. Remember that you are one, and all the reasons you fell in love with them in the first place. If you are going to be successful in conflict resolution, and marriage as a whole, you need to cultivate an environment of peace between one another.

Steps Toward Transparency

Transparency is crucial in marriage. If there are suppressed or ignored issues in marriage, don't be surprised if conflict arises as you discuss these topics! The longer you ignore an issue, the more it grows into something more serious. It's best to tackle these things together as they come up. When you do, you will find yourselves overcoming these hurdles much easier. Not only that, but you will also be developing further love, trust, and teamwork skills together as a result!

So, roll up your sleeves, become allies, and learn how to fight together for your relationship.

Giving a Blessing Instead of an Insult

The words we say are more powerful than we know. It's crucial that we only use kind, loving, and encouraging words to our spouse. We should strive in everything we saw to build up our spouse and not tear them down. God has given us our spouses as blessings in our lives. They are a gift, and we should be their partner in life in every way, working to help them prosper in every way in life.

Insulting your spouse is NEVER a good idea. The hurt that results from such an act is not easily, if ever, forgotten. One rash response from the person someone loves and has promised their entire life to can be more hurtful than most anything else in this life. A simple apology will not cover up for this offense. It takes a lot of time and work to regain trust to recover from such a hurtful mistake.

That's why, in conflict resolution, we should strive to give words of blessing to our spouses instead of insults. When talking through conflict, our first instinct should not be to defend ourselves but to honestly listen to the feelings of our spouse and seek to meet their needs in any way we can. We must have a heart that's open to change and compromise so that our marriage can thrive and we can build up our spouse as a result.

3 Things for Conflict Resolution

Knowing

If we are going to practice successful conflict resolution in our marriages, we must know our spouse. In the early days of our relationships, we spend a lot of time asking each other questions and getting to know one another. But how often do we continue this process throughout our marriages?

Now, this may sound silly at first. After being married for years, is there really anything else we could possibly learn about our spouses? Yes!

Absolutely! People are always changing and experiencing new things. Just think about it for a moment: you are not the same person you were when you first started dating or first got married, so why would you expect your spouse to be?

A beautiful part of marriage is the continual process of knowing one another. As you make that effort to connect with your spouse day after day, month after month, and year after year, you'll find yourself falling in love with them over and over again. This process will help you to quell conflicts as they arise.

Accepting

It's crucial that we accept our spouses for who they are. We are all flawed, imperfect human beings. We should not hold our spouses to unrealistic standards that we couldn't even live up to ourselves. Part of loving our spouse in a godly way involves embracing everything that makes them who they are!

Think about the way that you desire for your spouse to love and accept you unconditionally. That's exactly the kind of gift you should be giving to them as well! If you aren't willing to give it, don't expect to receive it.

When you love and accept your spouse without exceptions, you come to a place of understanding you've never been at before. This will help you talk through conflict instead of arguing or misunderstanding one another.

Adjusting

If we are to find loving and successful conflict resolution in our marriage, we must be willing to make adjustments in our mindset, plans, and feelings. If we are unmovable and firmly entrenched in our ways, it will only serve to stagnate or grow the conflict at hand.

No matter how close we are with our spouse, we are still two separate people with different identities, thoughts, feelings, and desires. Sometimes, these differences clash in a way where we need to adjust for one another. When we do, it shows our commitment and the selflessness of our love. When we don't, it causes hurt and puts a heavy strain on our marriage, making conflict resolution impossible.

Romans 12:18 says, *"Do all that you can to live in peace with everyone."* Now, if God expects us to strive to live at peace with everyone, how much more does He expect us to work hard at peace with our spouse?

Loving confrontation is the key. What do I mean by this? I mean that we must both confront conflict when it arises and do it with all love and patience. We mustn't gloss over conflict when it arises. It's important to handle it right away. But doing so doesn't mean we can do it in a loving way. We should never hurt or disrespect our spouse. That will never lead to a positive outcome in our attempts at conflict resolution.

There's a 3-Step process to practicing loving confrontation in conflict resolution:

Acknowledge the Hurt

Our first step in working toward conflict resolution is to acknowledge our own hurt and/or that of our spouse. If we don't take the time to recognize the hurt and the need for healing in the first place, how are we supposed to bring resolution to the conflict?

Examine the Offense

Next, we must examine the offense. What transpired that brought about the hurt? What about these particular circumstances was hurtful? How can this situation be avoided in the future? These are the kinds of questions we must ask when examining the offense.

What was my Contribution to the Problem

Last but not least, we must take an honest evaluation of our role in the problem. It's easy to deny our fault or to point fingers, but this is never fruitful. We must take ownership of whatever our role was in the situation in the first place. Sometimes, simply owning up to what you've done (or haven't done!) can be the first and most powerful first step to healing.

The 3 "Don'ts" of Conflict Resolution

Don't Compete

Marriage is NOT a competition. Competing in marriage is when we try to be "right" all the time in our marriage. We defend our opinions and feelings on things to the point where we lash out and cause conflict with our spouse. We place our own personal wants, feelings, and opinions on our spouse without truly listening to their side of everything.

When we fall into these types of patterns, we feel as if we are "competing" with our spouse. Instead of teaming together to conquer life, we try to do things our own way and on our own timing. This completely throws our marriages off-sync and doesn't allow space for the kind of unity and teamwork that make marriages thrive.

Don't Compare

It's easy to play the comparison game, but it's NEVER a good idea. Each person is different and every situation is different and we need to treat them as such. If we compare we are not making the effort to truly understand our spouse and their feelings. We must put in the effort to be a good and empathetic listener so we can understand what our partner is going through and find ways to meet their needs.

Don't Complain

Last but not least, don't complain! Complaining isn't loving and complaining doesn't solve anything. This means that complaining serves zero purpose in conflict resolution.

When we complain, all we are doing is attacking our spouse. Complaining means that we are airing out the things we don't like that our spouse has done but in a combative and unproductive manner. For instance, saying things like, "You never take out the trash!" This is the kind of complaining we must avoid at all times.

Sometimes, we may feel as if we are justified in complaining because we feel as if a wrong has been committed against us. Even if our spouse has done something wrong, complaining only serves to deepen the conflict, not solve it.

Weekly Meeting Questions

It's really helpful to have a weekly meeting session with your spouse to talk through any conflicts or potential conflicts from that week. Sometimes, this process can help you nip conflicts in the bud before they arise. Other times, they can provide the necessary and expected opportunity to talk through something one or both of you have been feeling. Always, these weekly meetings are an opportunity to connect, talk openly with one another, and grow stronger in communication.

Here are some great questions to ask one another as part of your time together:

1. **Have I offended you this week?**

2. **Is there an unmet need?**

3. **What are the priorities for the week?**

4. **How can I do better as a husband/wife this week?**

5. **What's your schedule this week?**

6. **How many times are we going to have relations this week?**

Living Out the Kindness of Christ

What do you think of when you hear the word "kindness?" Do you think of someone who always uses kind words? Or perhaps someone who typically goes out of their way to help others?

Kindness is so much more than simply being nice or pleasant to be around. Ephesians 4:32 says, *"Be kind and compassionate to one another, forgiving each other, just as in Christ God forgave you."* In this verse, kindness is likened to the forgiveness that we find in Jesus. Anyone has the capability to be nice, whether a follower of Christ or not. But kindness for those who proclaim Christ embodies so much more than what we normally think of when we hear this word.

In Biblical Greek, the word used for kindness denotes an idea of moral integrity and goodness. These are traits that also link this word back to Christ. We know that Jesus was the only person to ever have perfect moral integrity. He was the very definition of goodness. Every single positive thing that those words make up the very essence of who Jesus is. He lived out all of those things in every single thing He ever did.

When we think of kindness this way, it is the act of striving to show the love of Jesus in every encounter we have with our spouse. Kindness is working towards and seeking the good in your spouse. Instead of simply being about manners, kindness is about meeting the needs of your spouse before worrying about your own. When we live in that way, then we are truly displaying goodness in marriage.

When you live your marriage in this way, you are truly embodying the calling of Jesus and God's image within you. Commit to showing kindness and goodness toward your spouse, no matter the situation. In doing so, you will be the hands and feet of Jesus in their lives.

The Goodness of God

Psalm 31:19 says, *"How great is the goodness you have stored up for those who fear you. You lavish it on those who come to you for protection, blessing them before the watching world."*

The Bible begins with a beautiful story. The opening of the book of Genesis tells us the story of creation. God makes the world and everything in it. He tops it all off with His masterpiece: humanity made in His image. At the end of it all, God looks upon all He has done and declares that it is "very good." Creation moved on, imbued with God's goodness.

We know that the world has fallen since then and that things are not the same. But that doesn't mean that God doesn't still pour out His goodness upon us. We are His children, and He loves us more than we could ever understand. Just as we love to give everything we can to our kids, God is overjoyed in giving us everything He can.

And God's gifts are beyond anything we can comprehend. His goodness knows no bounds. That's why we are so abundantly blessed to be called His children. The blessings He floods our lives with are available nowhere else. If we live lives separate from God, we can never truly bloom into the people that we were created to be. That's because our lives were meant to be fueled by God's goodness.

We can live out His goodness and share it with our spouse through emulating Jesus Christ in everything we do. Embracing our identity in Christ helps us to realize the goodness that God placed inside of us. We honor God and spread His love when we go through our days striving to express

His image within us.

When you reflect God's goodness to your spouse, you love them in the way God is calling you to!

Biblical Example

The first couple we meet in the Bible is Adam and Eve. And guess what? We see them very early on experiencing conflict in their marriage. Even a couple who lived in the beautiful Garden of Eden found conflict arising between them!

Eve was deceived by the serpent and ate the forbidden fruit. Adam followed suit, them sharing equal responsibility in their sin. But what does Adam do when God confronts them about their misdeed? He begins to point fingers at his wife!

Now, you can imagine this didn't go over well with her at all, and you can't blame her! Instead of taking responsibility for their sin as a team, they both started pointing fingers. Adam blamed Eve, and Eve blamed the serpent. What they needed to do was be vulnerable and open with God about what they had done, but instead, they tried to cover their tracks. This only made things more difficult for them. They lost the blessing of the Garden and their relationship with God was fractured.

You can imagine all of this must have put a big strain on their relationship. If they would have simply been honest and upfront about the whole ordeal in the first place, they could have tackled this trial in their life as a team. Their love and support for one another would have helped them to see it all through with their heads held high.

Conflict puts a division between spouses in a place where there's supposed to be perfect unity and harmony. Conflict tears down peace between couples and replaces it with tension. Conflict erodes at love and pours resentment in its place.

How do we counter these effects before they get out of hand? Teamwork!

Ecclesiastes 4:9-12 reads,

Two are better than one, because they have a good return for their labor:

If either of them falls down, one can help the other up.

But pity anyone who falls and has no one to help them up.

Also, if two lie down together, they will keep warm.

But how can one keep warm alone?

Though one may be overpowered, two can defend themselves.

A cord of three strands is not quickly broken.

This verse is packed with wisdom regarding teamwork in marriage. Never look at conflict resolution as you trying to "fix" your spouse. Since you two have joined together in marriage, you are now one flesh. Take responsibility for whatever has occurred. Partner with your spouse in making things better, even if it was their actions that caused the rift in the first place.

What is this cord of three strands Ecclesiastes 4:12 speaks of? It is the union you and your spouse share with God. Not only are you unified with one another, but you must form a strong unity with God as well. Invite Him into your marriage, and in times of conflict, ask Him to spread His love between you and bring you to resolution. When the Lord is in the midst of your marriage, no conflict can tear you apart!

Your marriage is sacred. Commit to solving conflict as soon as it arises, as a TEAM through love and forgiveness. In conflict resolution, it's the small things that make all the difference. You don't have to totally change the way you interact with one another. It's more about how we manage one another than anything else.

At the end of the day, the only person you can change is yourself. You must hold yourself accountable for how you treat and respond to your spouse in times of conflict. You can control how they act or what they say, but you can set an example that can make all the difference.

We must flee from moral superiority. No "I hope you're listening" or any comments of that nature. In conflict resolution in marriage, we must continually strive for intentional, honest, and above all patient interaction with our spouse.

Confidentiality is essential when talking about sensitive issues with our spouse. If they have told you something that's only for you, then you best keep it that way. If you don't you will create a breach of trust that will have disastrous ripple effects throughout the rest of your marriage.

Don't judge or correct your spouse. You are not perfect yourself, so you have no place to be judging them. Instead, commit to helping each other to work toward becoming better together! We all have room to grow, and we should all accept our shortcomings and invite our spouse into that space so that we can grow into our best selves as a team. Then, instead of judgment, we will be able to give and receive unconditional support, love, and encouragement that will bring us to the next level, both individually and as a couple.

Reflection Questions:

1. Why is finger-pointing NEVER a good idea when trying to resolve conflict in marriage?

2. Read Ephesians 4:31-32 together. How does forgiveness form the foundation of sound conflict resolution in marriage? How can you work toward practicing forgiveness more diligently in your relationship?

Action Tips

➤ Sit down with your spouse and discuss conflict resolution. How have you handled it in the past? What have you done right? What can you do better? These are the types of questions you should ask one another.

➤ Commit to your spouse that you will NEVER finger point, use harsh words and that you will always practice forgiveness as Christ has called you to do.

➤ Discuss with your spouse what it means to be a team in marriage. Brainstorm ways that you can focus on developing yourselves as a better team going forward.

Scriptures for Reflection and Prayer

Ephesians 5:1: *"Follow God's example, therefore, as dearly loved children and walk in the way of love, just as Christ loved us and gave himself up for us as a fragrant offering and sacrifice to God."*

Hebrews 13:4: "*Give honor to marriage and remain faithful to one another in marriage.*"

Prayer

Lord, thank You for teaching us how to resolve conflict in a loving and godly way. We want nothing to ever come between us. Help us to develop our skills in conflict resolution so our love can endure and we can be stronger on the other side. Amen.

CHAPTER 2:

The Power of Forgiveness

"Forgiveness is freeing up and putting to
better use the energy once consumed by holding
grudges, harboring resentments, and nursing
unhealed wounds. It is rediscovering the
strengths we always had and relocating our
limitless capacity to understand and accept
other people and ourselves."

-Sidney and Suzanne Simon-

We had a friend come to us once, distraught over messages she had seen on her husband Jack's phone. She had discovered that he had been having inappropriate conversations with a coworker recently, and she was terrified that the cheating went beyond these conversations.

Thankfully, it didn't. Sadly, there was still a breach of trust and extreme hurt felt over the emotional unfaithfulness present in this situation. She had to have painful and open conversations with her husband. Not only that, but she had to hold back her anger and practice love, mercy, and forgiveness if she had any chance of salvaging her marriage.

Jack was apologetic, remorseful, and willing to repent and seek atonement for his sin. He was honest and straightforward about what had happened, and he earnestly desired to make things right. Thankfully, Leslie followed the Lord's leading and accepted his apology, and practiced forgiveness. He made the necessary steps and allowed himself to be held accountable going forward.

This powerful act of forgiveness saved their marriage, and after the hurt had healed, brought them closer together than ever before. She saw his dedication to change for the sake of their love, and he appreciated and was inspired by her bold and uncommon act of forgiveness.

Sadly, in every marriage, there will be times when one partner will have to seek forgiveness from the other, whether the offense committed was big or small.

Could you imagine what this situation would have looked like without forgiveness? Sadly, it's a common occurrence. Things like this rip apart marriages every day, and it's a tragedy. This is exactly why we need to embrace and practice bold and relentless forgiveness, even when it's challenging.

Forgiveness is necessary when someone has committed an injustice against you. That injustice has caused pain for one and potential guilt and remorse for the other. Both of these conditions need healing, a restoration that is only possible through the remarkable power of forgiveness.

Forgiveness is healing for both parties involved. For one, it relinquishes the pain that the other person has caused, that person deciding that they will let that pain hurt their heart no longer. For the other person, they are absolved of guilt and able to walk forward in life. For both, they get to experience a renewed and rejuvenated relationship.

Jesus' redemptive work of love on the cross was the ultimate act of forgiveness and look how it changed the world! How could a loving act of forgiveness change your marriage?

If Jesus was willing to forgive us all for the multitude of sins we've committed, what excuse do we have not to forgive our spouse?

When God's Word tells us to forgive, it's not a suggestion: it is a commandment from God Himself. Forgiveness is so much more than it may seem on the surface. It has innumerable benefits that can be found nowhere else. Forgiveness has the power to elevate relationships to previously unattainable levels. Forgiveness has the power to bring healing to broken hearts. And most importantly, forgiveness has the influence to rob evil of its power over us.

How is that you may ask? Let's look towards Jesus' example, as we should in everything. When Jesus took on the full force of death on the cross and rose from the dead, He denied evil's power over Him. He took everything the enemy had to dish out and still got up from it.

And what was His entire sacrifice meant to accomplish? Forgiveness for sins for the entire human race. Jesus took death on a cross so that the necessary price could be paid for every evil thing we have done in the past and will do in the future. It was through forgiveness that Jesus broke the power of evil in this world.

It's through forgiveness that we likewise can dispel the effects of evil in our lives. When you forgive someone, you are releasing both you and them from the burden their offense brought into being. You are looking the evil committed against you in the face and denying it any power over you. Through the sacrificial work of Jesus, you have that power. Never forget it.

We have all had to forgive our spouses for something they have done at one point or another. But sometimes forgiveness isn't as easy as saying "I forgive you" because you truly have let all the hurt, resentment, or anger go; the offense is still there waiting for them to do something else wrong so you can bring up all the other offenses they've committed in the past.

We must avoid this tendency at all costs. Ephesians 4:32 reads, *"Make a clean break with all cutting, backbiting, profane talk. Be gentle with one another, sensitive. Forgive one another as quickly and thoroughly as God in Christ forgave you"* (MSG). The Bible urges us toward gentleness and love because all of the cutting, backbiting, and profane talk does incredible damage to a relationship. When we give in to it, all we are doing is letting the enemy win. The devil wants to see godly marriages broken up. So, when we give into our sinful human nature and fight with one another, we are just furthering the devil's plans and not God's. Is that what we really want?

Absolutely not, because we are children of God! We want to build each other up and become as strong as we possibly can as a team. Then, together, we can pursue God's will for our lives and join as one in the blessed work of furthering God's Kingdom here on the earth. God has a divine purpose for each person and every marriage. As a married couple under the Lord, we can seek and fulfill those purposes like never before, but we have to be living out our marriage in loving unity to succeed.

Forgiveness means…

No Looking Back

Looking back on previous struggles or offenses is NEVER fruitful. All this does is distract from resolving the conflict at hand, either starting or escalating an argument. Doing this is akin to throwing gas on a fire: it will get out of hand quickly!

Truly forgiving your spouse means that you NEVER bring up something you've forgiven them about. If you do, have you truly forgiven them? Or are you still holding on to resentment all this time? Forgiveness means taking any feelings of resentment and casting them away forever.

Not Keeping a List

Some will keep a list of everything their spouse has ever done wrong, ready to hurl it at them the moment a conflict arises, and they feel the need to defend themselves. It's that attitude of, "Hey, I know I did this, but look at all the stuff YOU do!" This is a selfish and unhelpful tactic that only deepens conflict within our marriages.

When you practice true forgiveness with your spouse, it means the forgiven offense is gone FOREVER. You are making a commitment to never bring it up again and to leave it in the past where it belongs. If we truly want to grow in our marriages, we have to continually look toward the future and not the past.

Refusing to Carry Bitterness or Resentment

Bitterness and resentment are dangerous things. They take root in our hearts, growing and festering there until they are completely out of our control. They serve no healthy or productive purposes in our lives or marriage.

Holding on to those kinds of feelings creates unhealthy barriers between us and our spouse. It breaks down emotional intimacy between a couple and inhibits meaningful connection. We must release these feelings when they arise, fighting against them any time they rear their ugly heads.

Living Each Day Free of Bad Memories

Forgiveness is deeply healing, both to you and to your spouse who you've forgiven. Through forgiveness, you are telling your spouse that they are more important to you than whatever hurt you are feelings. It is a powerful way to demonstrate how your marriage is more precious to you than anything else. You'd rather be united and growing in love with your spouse than simply being "right."

When you do this, you allow yourself and your spouse to move forward and live each and every day free of bad memories. All of the pain, anger, and resentment turns into love for one another and hope for the future. Forgiveness and the freedom it brings can change our whole perspective, and in turn, save our marriages!

Look to the Future with Hope (Being Optimistic that your Spouse won't Repeat the same Offense)

After forgiving your spouse and moving on, it can be hard not to be worried that the same thing will transpire again. Sometimes, we put our guards up and even though we've forgiven our spouse, we are still cautious in certain ways with them. While this is understandable, especially in particularly hurtful situations, it is not fruitful or healthy for you and your spouse.

If we don't believe in our spouse to change and be better going forward, they will pick up on it. That won't be encouraging to them at all! If they are struggling with something that had caused them to act in the way they did in the first place, it's our role to walk alongside them and help them to overcome whatever it is they may be facing. We must be their biggest support through their journey, and that means being optimistic and putting our trust in them.

Why Don't People Forgive their Spouse?

Sometimes, someone may feel as if they are encouraging him or her by condoning the action/offense. They don't want their spouse to think that what they did wasn't hurtful or impactful to their life. They want their spouse to feel the weight of their actions and the pain it has brought upon them. While this makes sense, and some would say is understandable, it's not the way to go.

It is completely appropriate to express to your spouse how their words or actions have hurt you. You want to be open and honest about the impact their offense has had on you. But there's a right and wrong way to go about it. Instead of attacking your spouse and trying to cause additional pain, tell them sternly about your feelings but still offer forgiveness. Let them know how much they hurt you, but also let them know that your love and commitment is stronger than the pain they have caused you.

You may be hesitant to forgive because you might feel you're setting yourself up for the same thing to happen again. You can let your spouse know that even though you've forgiven them, their behavior was unacceptable and that you expect it not to happen going forward. Ask them what they need to make sure it doesn't happen again and offer your support to encourage them in that process. If there's a need they have that you can meet, be committed to meeting it.

Remember forgiveness doesn't make the other person right; it makes you free! It's not about being right or wrong. Marriage is not a competition. You can't wait for your spouse to deserve it or ask for it. You should do it because God forgives you. Offering forgiveness, especially when your spouse doesn't even seek or deserve it, can be the most impactful thing you can do.

Forgiveness is a choice; it's not that you can't do it: you choose not to do it!

Colossians 3:13 says, *"Bear with each other and forgive one another if any of you has a grievance against someone. Forgive as the Lord forgave you."*

I ask you this: how did the Lord forgive you? Jesus went to the cross to die on behalf of us. Before he even made it to the cross, He was beaten within an inch of His life, humiliated, and tortured mentally, physically, spiritually, and emotionally. He knew exactly what He was facing going in, and He did it anyway. Why? Because He knew that this was what it would take for YOU to experience forgiveness! And even though we are all sinful and didn't ask for this forgiveness or deserve it, He extended it to us anyway.

Pray over this truth and let it really sink in. Now, that's precisely the kind of grace and forgiveness God expects you to extend to your spouse: free, loving, and sometimes self-sacrificing love, grace, and forgiveness.

Jesus doesn't mince words on the topic of forgiveness. In Matthew 6:15 He says, "*If you do not forgive others their sins, your Father will not forgive your sins.*" That is crystal clear. He does not say to forgive when it is easy to forgive. He doesn't give a list of unforgiveable things. He simply says to forgive, no matter what the offense may be.

Forgiveness has a way of diffusing anger, which escalates conflict and leads to broken relationships. Proverbs 10:12 says, "*Hatred stirs up conflict, but love covers over all wrongs.*" When we counter anger with love, we save relationships. Not only that, but we help them to grow deeper. The kind of love that it takes to forgive your spouse is the same kind of love that becomes a catalyst to taking your relationship to the next level.

When God's Word tells us to forgive, it's not a suggestion: it is a commandment from God Himself. Ephesians 4:32 says, "*Be kind and compassionate to one another, forgiving each other, just as in Christ God forgave you.*"

Forgiveness is so much more than it may seem on the surface. It has innumerable benefits that can be found nowhere else. Forgiveness has the power to elevate relationships to previously unattainable levels. Forgiveness has the power to bring healing to broken hearts. And most importantly, forgiveness has the influence to rob evil of its power over us.

How is that you may ask? Let's look towards Jesus' example, as we should in everything. When Jesus took on the full force of death on the cross and rose from the dead, He denied evil's power over Him. He took everything the enemy had to dish out and still got up from it.

And what was His entire sacrifice meant to accomplish? Forgiveness for sins for the entire human race. Jesus took death on a cross so that the necessary price could be paid for every evil thing we have done in the past and will do in the future. It was through forgiveness that Jesus broke the power of evil in this world.

It's through forgiveness that we likewise can dispel the effects of evil in our lives. When you forgive your spouse, you are releasing both you and them from the burden their offense brought into being. You are looking the evil committed against you in the face and denying it any power over you. Through the sacrificial work of Jesus, you have that power. Never forget it.

Forgiveness is necessary when your spouse has committed an offense against you. That injustice has caused pain for one and potential guilt and remorse for the other. Both of these conditions need healing, a restoration that is only possible through the remarkable power of forgiveness.

Forgiveness is healing for both you and your spouse. For one, it relinquishes the pain that the other person has caused, that person deciding that they will let that pain hurt their heart no longer. For your spouse, they are absolved of guilt and able to walk forward in life. For both, they get to experience a renewed and rejuvenated relationship.

Jesus' redemptive work of love on the cross was the ultimate act of forgiveness and look how it changed the world! How could a loving act of forgiveness change your marriage?

If Jesus was willing to forgive us all for the multitude of sins we've committed, what excuse do we have not to forgive our spouse?

This is why we must master confession and forgiveness. We can learn everything we need to know on this through **1 Corinthians 13:4**:

"Love endures with patience and serenity, love is kind and thoughtful, and is not jealous or envious; love does not brag and is not proud or arrogant. It is not rude; it is not self-seeking, it is not provoked [nor overly sensitive and easily angered]; it does not take into account a wrong endured. It does not rejoice at injustice, but rejoices with the truth [when right and truth prevail]. Love bears all things [regardless of what comes], believes all things [looking for the best in each one], hopes all things [remaining steadfast during difficult times], endures all

things [without weakening]. Love never fails [it never fades nor ends]" (AMP).

I can't stress enough the importance of forgiveness. **Ephesians 4:31-32** says, *"Get rid of all bitterness, rage and anger, brawling and slander, along with every form of malice. Be kind and compassionate to one another, forgiving each other, just as in Christ God forgave you."* Forgiveness is the foundation of conflict resolution. Without it, the conflict will never be truly resolved.

When you look at the story of the Gospel, the central message of our faith, it all centers around forgiveness. God loved us so much that He gave up His beloved Son on a cross to bring us salvation through the unmatched power of forgiveness. Through that forgiveness, do you know what happens? Our relationship with God is restored.

In the same way, when you practice forgiveness with your spouse, your relationship with them will likewise be restored.

Forgiveness is all about looking injustice and evil in the face and denying its power over you. If your spouse has committed a sin against you, forgiveness is the declaration that you are not going to let the effects of that action dominate your life and marriage. Forgiveness is the commitment to healing and casting our hurt, pain, and anger into the hands of the Lord. If we hold on to these things, they will only grow within us until they are out of control. Forgiveness will allow us to move on, bringing healing to both us and our spouse.

Reflection Questions

1. How does love diffuse anger? How can this help our marriages to grow and not be suffocated by the pain of an offense?

2. How is forgiveness at the heart of the Gospel? What does that mean for why we are to practice radical forgiveness in our marriage?

Action Tips:

➢ Commit to forgiving your spouse, no matter their offense.

➢ Have a conversation with your spouse about forgiveness and the role it plays in the Gospel and in your marriage. Make it a time of fellowship and connection.

➢ Share with your spouse a time when forgiveness had a big impact on your life. Listen to their stories as well.

Scripture for Prayer and Reflection:

Ephesians 4:32: *"Be kind to each other, tenderhearted, forgiving one another, just as God through Christ has forgiven you."*

Matthew 6:15: *"If you refuse to forgive others, your Father will not forgive your sins."*

Proverbs 10:12: *"Hatred stirs up quarrels, but love makes up for all offenses."*

Proverbs 17:9 *"Love prospers when a fault is forgiven, but dwelling on it separates close friends."*

Prayer

Lord, forgiveness can be hard. When hurt comes from someone you have placed all your love and trust in, it's hard to let go of it. Grant me Your power so that I can forgive my spouse, releasing both of us from the pain between us. I long to move forward and have a stronger marriage than ever before. I know this is possible through You. Amen.

CHAPTER 3:

Finding Balance

"God gave us a spirit not of fear but of power
and love and self-control."

-2 Timothy 1:7-

A car is made out of many individual parts that work together toward a common goal. Take the wheels off your car, and no matter how healthy the engine is, you aren't going anywhere! Your car needs balance and alignment between all its components to operate in the way it's intended to.

The same is true of our marriages. There are many factors ever-present in the life of any couple. If these things are not in balance and alignment, your marriage will not be running at the level it was intended to.

Key Identifiers that Your Relationship is Out of Alignment

1. Is your partner spending more time with their friends than you?

2. Does your significant other spend money with no regard, but they want to dictate your spending?

3. Do you find yourself saying "No" to friends' invitations to go out? But your partner isn't doing the same.

4. Are you continually giving in to things you don't really want to do?

   Example: You always defer when you head out to eat, and your partner asks, "What are you in the mood for?" do you reply, "I don't know.

What are you in the mood for?" or, "Whatever you want"?

5. **Does your significant other only call you when it is convenient for him or her?**

   Example: On the way back from work or while waiting for the bus? Do you always answer the phone because you don't want to miss the person's call? Maybe you're okay with that, but if it's not a good time for you, don't answer the phone. Call back later when it is more convenient for you.

6. **Does your significant other have a temper and feel it's their right to take it out on you? Or do you quietly listen to them venting because it "isn't a big deal"?**

   Guess what? It is. If you don't like a person's tone or volume, just tell them to stop yelling, venting, complaining, blaming you, etc. If they don't stop, say it again, and if that doesn't help, walk out of the room or hang up the phone. You have to set up healthy boundaries and expectations for how your spouse treats you. If you don't, they aren't likely to change their behavior.

What is a Balanced Relationship?

You must see yourself as an equal member and be treated the same way. Finding Balance in a relationship involves two individuals making a conscious effort to build a positive relationship. A healthy relationship is about giving and taking. The involved individuals need to contribute and receive the same amount of support and assurance.

10 Ways to Maintain Balance in a Relationship

1. Communicate

Each partner must be comfortable expressing their feelings to the other. Anything lesser than this will result in an uneven relationship.

Without open lines of two-way communication, the relationship will be out of balance because only one partner is really being heard and considered.

The whole point of a relationship is to co-create an environment where both people complement each other. If each person isn't contributing or isn't able to contribute, the relationship will likely be one-sided.

2. Accept Disagreement

Having a balanced relationship doesn't mean you agree on everything – in fact, it can be just the opposite. We may think that disagreements are a bad thing, but that's not always the case! We are all unique individuals with our own perspectives, beliefs, and experiences. Even though we are one in marriage, we still maintain our individuality as well. Accepting these disagreements and respecting each other's differences actually goes a long way in promoting love and unity between you.

3. Respect Your Partner's Wishes

Another effective way to create a balanced relationship is to respect your partner's wishes and decisions. There are moments when your partner will make decisions you aren't comfortable with. The best thing to do is to accept it without making a big deal out of it.

It does not matter if they are taking the wrong step. Yes! It can be painful watching your partner make a wrong decision when you can stop them. However, you can't do much if they don't want your help. All you can do is advise them and allow them to make a choice.

Also, when they make mistakes, do not rub them in their face by saying, "I told you so." A balanced relationship means the partners must be empathetic towards each other.

When the world turns against your partner, you should be their safe space. Instead of judging them, it is best to find solutions together. You can strengthen and build one another up in a way no one else can.

4. Build Trust in Your Relationship

If you want to know how to maintain a balance in your relationship, you must be reliable and trust your partner. It is sometimes hard to trust, especially if you have been betrayed in the past. But you can't take it out on your new partner if you want a balanced relationship. To build trust in your relationship, try to be reliable by keeping to your words.

Honesty is one of the key ingredients in building trust in a relationship. Strive to be truthful with your partner in all situations, big and small. What you think is a small or "white lie" is still at its core a lie. Once you are caught telling a lie, it is challenging for your partner to trust you again. Do what you say, and don't go back on your words.

5. Be Authentically You/Be Yourself

If your relationship is going to have true balance, you both need to be authentic. "Any time you are not authentically yourself it's a sign that you are not truly comfortable in a relationship," relationship therapist Aimee Hartstein, LCSW tells Bustle. "If you are hiding things, embarrassed about things, faking things, it suggests that you don't feel that [your partner] will truly like you for yourself."

If you are to have a balanced relationship, you have to feel comfortable being yourself! Being fake with your partner will only put up walls between you in terms of connection, communication, and intimacy.

6. Consult and Consider Each Other in Decision-Making

You might not always do what the other one wants, but having a balanced relationship means taking them into consideration. If only one of you is thinking about the other, there's no balance. You should both be taking each other's needs into account in every decision you make. Both of your wants and needs should be important to one another!

It's important to serve our spouses at all times. When we put the needs of our spouses above our own, we honor both our spouse and God. When we do this, we meet each other's needs. Be a servant of your spouse at all times. There are few greater ways you can show your love.

7. Be Independent / Don't be too Dependent on your Partner

Nonetheless, it is best not to rely on your partner for everything. That's because your partner can get overwhelmed and the perception can form that you can't stand on your own.

Having a balanced relationship isn't just about balance between the two of you, it's also about having balance between your relationship and the rest of your life. "It's incredibly important for both partners to maintain a sense of independence outside of their relationship," Jalesa Tucker, a content coordinator at One Love, a foundation dedicated to teaching young people about healthy and unhealthy relationships, tells Bustle. "By engaging in activities independent of each other, couples are better able to maintain their sense of self and bring diverse experiences to their relationship."

8. Fleeing from Pride

Realizing your strength does not mean being prideful. Love does not seek to make itself known! Rather, we are called to have a healthy understanding of our strengths and weaknesses. God desires for us to be confident, yet humble, giving credit to Him in all things for He is the author of all our victories. This kind of humbleness, the opposite of pride, is a key ingredient of being a successful spouse.

How do we achieve this? One of the best things you can do as you go through life, faith, and marriage is to know yourself. What do I mean by that? Knowing yourself means that you have a solid grasp and understanding of your strengths, weaknesses, and triggers. The truth of the matter is that we're all unique and struggle with different things. There are different feelings, situations, and distractions that will throw one person off their God-given path. That's why it's essential to know what those things are for us!

When we do, it helps us to put our lives into perspective. We can more clearly see where our decisions are leading us and what might or might not be the best choice forward in any given situation. It brings a lot of inner peace to know yourself because you don't have to constantly question what you're doing and why you're doing it. You have an understanding of yourself and what you're all about that drives you forward in life according to your firm convictions.

This is so important because our enemy, Satan, looks to feed off of our vulnerabilities. He knows them very well and will exploit them in an effort to make us fall prey to his deceptions. Never doubt the reality of the devil and his schemes. 1 Peter 5:8 shows us the seriousness of Satan's great evil and his persistence in attacking the children of God: "Stay alert! Watch out for your great enemy, the devil. He prowls around like a roaring lion, looking for someone to devour."

Satan is against everything that is of God. He wants nothing more than to derail God's plans at any cost. He is the antithesis of everything that God is. We were created in the image of God, so that means that he's out for us as well! He might try to deceive us and have us believe that he's leading us somewhere good for us, but never be fooled: he wishes only to lead us to destruction.

If we don't have a solid grasp of our identity and purpose, we will struggle in marriage. If we don't know who we are and what God has called us to do, we will not be running at full capacity for our spouse like they deserve!

9. The Common Enemy of Anxiety

In today's world, anxiety is the enemy of many. It affects people without prejudice, growing and festering within us until it's nearly impossible for us to control. With our overburdened schedules and isolated lives, anxiety has many opportunities to enter our hearts.

Anxiety is all about the fear of the unknown, but we must never fear what is ahead. We live by faith and not by sight! While our perspective is limited, God can see all. As His children, He is leading our lives. We can trust in Him to guide us precisely where we need to be.

When we walk with Jesus through life, He will guard our hearts and minds. We must rest our burdens upon His shoulders, and He will grant us peace that leads us through the most challenging times of our lives. With our faith firmly planted in Him, Jesus gives us power over anxiety.

We must fight the anxiety that plagues us at all costs. Anxiety is the opposite of faith. The more that anxiety comes to take residence in our hearts, the less room there is for faith to dwell there. In order to grow a rich and vibrant faith, we must let our trust in the Lord and His promises outweigh the anxiety in our hearts. There is no worry too big in this world that we cannot place in God's hands!

We need to help one another along this journey as a couple. The better we are both feeling mentally, the better we will both be able to live out God's vision for our marriage. Always lend an ear to your spouse and be there for them to give them your support when they need you most.

10. Realizing Your Strength

In Psalm 27:3, David writes "Though an army may encamp against me, my heart shall not fear; Though war may rise against me, in this I will be confident." King David wrote these words with a heavy burden on his heart. An army of his enemies lay before his Kingdom with violent intent against God's people. David had been charged by God with the responsibility to defend them. It was a heavy burden for him, but through God's power he delivered the people from those who would harm them.

There are times we have battles of our own to fight in life. This will undoubtedly happen in the life of every couple. But through the influence of the Holy Spirit that lives inside of us, we become mighty warriors in Christ. He equips us with every tool we need to be confident and victorious in spiritual warfare against the weapons of the enemy.

Embrace your role as a warrior of God's Kingdom. Commit to fighting the onslaught of sin in your life and in the world. It is a great responsibility, but we are blessed to be able to carry it out in Christ's name. Focus on the spiritual disciplines of Bible-reading, prayer and fellowship. All of them will help prepare you for the battles that are to come. If you and your spouse do this together, you will find the strength you need by finding balance according to the standard of God's Word.

Reflection Questions

1. Why is it important to find balance in your marriage?

2. How does not having balance negatively affect your relationship?

Action Tips

➢ Have an open and honest conversation with your spouse. Ask one another questions such as, "Is our relationship in balance?" If not, strategize and make goals in key areas you need to work on together.

➢ Make a list of the past five decisions you've had to make as a couple. Did you make them together? Or did one of you make the decision without consulting the other? Talk through what you find.

Scriptures for Prayer and Reflection

2 Timothy 1:7: *"God gave us a spirit not of fear but of power and love and self-control."*

Matthew 6:24: *"No one can serve two masters. For you will hate one and love the other; you will be devoted to one and despise the other. "*

Prayer

Lord, life and relationships are all about balance. Thank You for teaching us this and help us to live out a balanced marriage. We wish this so we can thrive in love, both for one another and for You. Amen.

CHAPTER 4:

˙Running on Empty

"Those who trust in the Lᴏʀᴅ will find new strength. They will soar high on wings like eagles. They will run and not grow weary. They will walk and not faint."

-Isaiah 40:31-

Lasting love is like taking a lifelong road trip. Many of us get lost during our journey. Maybe we take a wrong turn by saying something mean, and in our own hurt we avoid making an attempt to turn back around to get on the right road again. Eventually, our relationship runs out of gas, and we become stranded.

The Empty Love Tank

We all need love and affection from our spouses. Some may need it more or less, or in different ways, but it is a need for all of us in marriage. When we don't get it at all or in the ways that speak to us, we can lash out. Hostility, criticism, and demands are really cries for emotional connection. Couples with lasting and happy relationships have a strong friendship, intimately know each other, and have more positive moments of connection than negative. They know one another's love language and speak to it in meaningful ways.

As humans, we are wired to connect with other people and when we are disconnected, we suffer immensely. We feel empty, lonely, and broken. What is the cruelest punishment in the world? The answer is solitary confinement; complete disconnection from other humans. This is why we must learn how to get the love we need and how to give the love our partner needs when we ask how to make a relationship last.

Your Relationship's Love Tank

In Dr. Gary Chapman's popular book, The Five Love Languages, he writes that every person has a Love Tank. I would like to propose that every relationship has its own Love Tank.

A couple's Love Tank is filled by the frequency of emotional connections and is drained by the ways a couple disconnects. In your daily life, there are events that fill up your Love Tank. These include emotional and physical affection, your partner asking about your day, helping out with laundry, and weekly dates. Your partner's Love Tank also gets filled up in ways that are sometimes similar, sometimes different.

Consider a car for a moment. It has a tank of its own, a gas tank. If that tank is empty, the car will not run. Even if the tank is running low, driving for too long like that can cause long-term damage to your vehicle. You have to make sure you are continually filling your car's gas tank. In the same way, we must always do things that fill up our love tank if we desire for our marriage to run at its full potential.

It's crucial that we take the time to learn and understand the things that fill up the love tanks of ourselves, our spouse, and our marriage. Then, we will know exactly how to fill them and avoid the complications that arise from running on empty.

Things That Empty The Love Tank

-Work stress

-Unresponsive partner

-Unresolved conflict

-Broken trust

-Lack of affection

-Other forms of disconnection that drain your energy.

Some incidents drain your Love Tank faster than others. Some events that empty our Love Tank may be negative at first but can actually improve a relationship over time. Conflict is a great example. You may have a difficult argument that is stressful and tense, but the end result is a greater amount in the Love Tank than the initial amount drained. You actually learned how to love your partner better and they learned how to love you better—that produces connection to refill your Love Tank.

During this conflict, you may have resolved an important issue which will bring you closer and create a deeper sense of we-ness. These events may have a positive result in the end, but are still outputs that require inputs, such as a repair, to deepen a romantic bond and fill up a relationship's Love Tank.

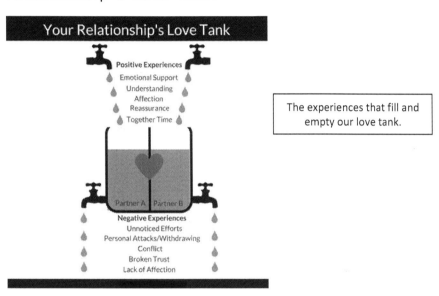

The experiences that fill and empty our love tank.

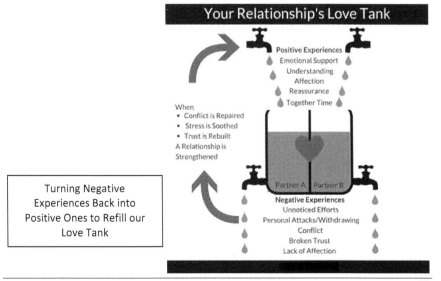

Turning Negative Experiences Back into Positive Ones to Refill our Love Tank

Key Takeaways

- The positive moments of connection must exceed the negative moments of connection to maintain a full Love Tank.

- Negative moments drain a Love Tank faster than positive moments fill it up.

- There's a fine balance to maintain in a positive relationship.

- When a Love Tank is draining, insecurity enters a relationship and even the most confident partners can feel insecure.

- When this happens, partners run for cover or criticize if they feel unappreciated, unwanted, or mistreated. That's why it's so important to practice giving some kind of reassurance daily. Do tiny actions daily that display commitment, love, and affection.

  o Tell your significant other that you love them.

  o Buy their favorite candy bar and surprise them.

  o Soothe their insecurities with kindness and care instead of defensiveness.

By filling up your partner's Love Tank, you'll make them feel secure, important, and loved. As a result, you'll receive a lot more support in making the relationship last.

Keeping Your Love Tank Full

As Dr. Sue Johnson says, "Love is a constant process of tuning in, connecting, missing and misreading cues, disconnecting, repairing and finding deeper connection. It's a dance of meeting and parting and finding each other again. Minute-to-minute and day-to-day."

You have two options:

1. **Refill and Repair your Love Tank on a Daily Basis**

   a. That means intentionally reconnecting, listening to each other's happy and difficult emotions, being supportive, and making time for the relationship.

2. **Let the Relationship Problems Accumulate and Drain your Tank**

   a. Once you hit empty, your heart will force you to give up on the relationship or seek out couple's therapy.

Repairing and Reconnecting is Required for Lasting Love

No matter who you love, there are going to be misunderstandings, hurt feelings, and moments of disconnection. A Love Tank will have leaks and drain from time to time. That is natural. When it happens, it's ok! It's not time to freak out, but it is good to recognize so you can make the necessary repairs.

The difference between couples who maintain a full Love Tank and those who don't is their willingness to repair and reconnect in order to make a relationship last. Some will fight hard to repair their tank so that they can continue to experience the immensely powerful relationship they started off with. Some will sadly let their tank fall into disrepair until the point it's too late. Remember, a full love tank equals a secure relationship!

Reflection Questions

1. What is a "love tank" and why is it important to your marriage?

2. Before reading this chapter, were you familiar with the concept of love languages? If not, how has it enlightened you to how to meet the needs of your spouse?

Action Tips

> Take out a piece of paper and write down what fills your emotional tank. Also write down what drains your emotional tank. Share it with your spouse.

> Have a conversation with your spouse about your love languages. Ask them which resonates with them the most. Share your

love language as well. Strategize on how you can meet each other's needs through your individual love languages.

Prayer

Lord, fill us with the patience and love to not only learn what fills our love tank but to give those things to our partner. A little bit of listening can go a long way, so help us to be better listeners to each other. We want to meet each other's needs and fill our love tank to the brim. Amen.

CHAPTER 5:

Tune Up: Communication

"Communication is the lifeline of any
relationship."

-Elizabeth Bourgeret-

You've heard the saying, "Communication is key," and you're likely sick of having it shoved down your throat! But there's a reason why it's such a tried-and-true saying: It's the 100%, unadulterated truth. Your level of intimate, open, and honest communication with your spouse will make or break your relationship.

We knew a couple who seemed to have it all together. From the outside, it looked like they had it made. They had great jobs, a beautiful home, and two lovely children. Suddenly, out of the blue to those on the outside, they announced they were getting a divorce. What could have possibly gone wrong?

Turns out it wasn't sudden at all. Everything we were seeing from the outside was just a front covering up a marriage starved of communication and quality time with one another. This distance between husband and wife grew and grew until they didn't even know one another anymore.

It was tragic: They were no longer engaged and part of each other's lives. In their personal life, they did their own things. Family time was simply for the sake of the kids. Work was work, and neither spoke into the other's challenges there. These two people who got married while they were madly in love had turned into mere strangers.

I can't tell you how many couples I've spoken with that have come to me with their relationship woes, seemingly dumbfounded on how to resolve them. As we continue talking and I glean information about the nature of their relationship, I realize quickly that they rarely communicate or spend time together! No wonder things aren't going well!

Here's a simple summary of what's going on here and listen closely: if you don't communicate with one another and don't spend quality time together, your relationship will suffer for it. Relationships are built upon a foundation of strong communication and quality time with one another.

What the Bible Says

Abraham and Sarah were a biblical couple that showed us clearly the challenges that arise when we don't communicate with our spouses. They were a godly couple, no doubt, and the Bible makes clear of that. But they didn't handle every situation well, leaving us a powerful lesson to learn from regarding communication.

Abraham and Sarah desired to have children. It was a genuine, beautiful, and earnest desire that was rooted in God. But yet, Sarah was barren: She could have no children. For any of those who have experienced such a time in their lives, it is pure torture. You feel as if you have been robbed of the most beautiful thing in the world, and it's incredibly hard to wait on God's timing for the answer He has yet to give you.

That's precisely where Abraham and Sarah found

themselves. Their desire to bear children burned strong, but no children came. But God heard their cries and spoke into their pain. He promised that Sarah would bear a child!

Now, you would think that Abraham and Sarah would be over the moon. But instead, Sarah laughed at God. Why? Because she had been so absorbed by her grief that she doubted the power of God. She thought that because she was much older now such a thing wouldn't even be possible. She had forgotten that God can do all things, regardless of what we believe to be possible.

Because of her disbelief, she makes a terrible mistake. She hands off their maidservant to her husband so that she could bear a child for them. Now, they didn't talk this one through. Abraham merely accepts his wife's proposal, and their servant bears them a child. This would lead to a chain of events that would cause an immense amount of strain within their marriage. Could you imagine being in such a situation? It's a sure-fire recipe for conflict to explode!

Even through all of this, God was faithful to His promises. Sarah conceived and bore a son, even in her advanced age. If they had simply communicated in the first place, reminded each other of God's promise, and clung to faith as a team, they could have avoided so much pain.

How to Communicate

Not only is communicating important, but also *how* we communicate. Proverbs 12:18 says, "*The words of the reckless pierce like swords, but the tongue of the wise brings healing.*" Your words have the power to empower your spouse or tear them down. The way that you choose to speak into their life is all up to you.

Remember, it's much better to avoid hurtful words altogether than to apologize for them later. While forgiveness is real and needed, the wounds from hurtful words take time to heal. Do you want to inflict such pain on the person you love enough to have devoted your life to in front of your family, friends, and God Himself?

Instead, let your words become a wellspring of life within your spouse. Speak into their life in empowering ways. Encourage them in their work and hobbies; point out their best qualities; tell them they are beautiful/handsome on a daily basis; and most importantly of all, tell them you love them daily! You'd be amazed at how many couples have forgotten even those basic and cherished words of affection.

The Bible continually warns us about not speaking in hurtful ways. **Colossians 3:8** says, "*Now you must also rid yourselves of all such things as these: anger, rage, malice, slander, and filthy language from your lips.*" If you tend to struggle with the types of things listed in Colossians 3:8, it's something that you must commit to working on right away. Seek help from a spiritual mentor or counselor if necessary. There is no shame in asking for help: In fact, it's admirable to make the bold steps necessary to better ourselves!

If you find yourself within the midst of a communication and quality time-starved marriage, you're likely experiencing conflict because of it. To resolve that conflict, you must start at the roots of the issue as we have discussed in this chapter.

First of all, carve out time for each other every day. It doesn't matter how you do it, as long as you commit to it and stick to it. Set expectations that it will be a time to truly connect in all honesty and vulnerability with one another. Tell each other about your day, do an activity together you both enjoy, cook dinner together…whatever you decide to do, make it something mutually beneficial that will draw you closer to one another.

Also, make the commitment to one another to speak only words of love and empowerment into each other's lives. Hold each other accountable to this and make sure it is mutual. Look for ways that you can speak into each other's lives daily in profound and powerful ways.

When you do these things, you will see the conflict in your marriage lessen dramatically! And not only that, when conflict does arise, because of your newfound communication skills, you'll be able to handle it quickly and efficiently instead of letting it cause a rift between you.

Listen to Understand, Not to Respond

Effective listening goes beyond hearing someone's words. Effective listening creates an environment where the other person feels that you understand them.

This tip applies to attitude more than it does to behavior. Many people view dialogue like a tennis match where the two parties square off and hit the ball back-and-forth. In this approach to conversation, both parties are adversaries trying to "score the point."

To listen effectively, I suggest that you view dialogue more like a pitcher and catcher in a baseball game. The pitcher (speaker) throws the ball for the catcher (you) to receive it. The catcher only throws the ball back after he has it firmly in his grasp.

In other words, listen to receive the meaning. Once you understand, then you can respond.

Be Quiet

Being quiet gives you the opportunity to hear the words, the tone, and the meaning behind the words. It gives you the chance to observe the speaker's body language.

To help you remember this tip, I'll share two quick statements with you:

- "When your mouth is open, your ears are closed."

- "LISTEN and SILENT have the same letters."

Let Them Finish Their Thoughts

In other words, don't interrupt the speaker. From the previous tip, this idea seems obvious. However, I have seen many arguments and misunderstandings that stemmed from interruptions. It's hard to remain silent. It's even harder to remain silent until someone has completely expressed their idea.

Maintain Eye Contact

Effective listening means observing everything about the speaker's message. People communicate at least as much with their body language as they do with their words. Good listeners learn to "listen" with their eyes as well as with their ears.

If you choose to work on something else (answer e-mail, fill out paperwork, etc.) while your spouse is speaking to you, they will not "feel" that they were heard.

Ask questions to ensure that you understand

Just because you heard the words and observed the body language, don't assume that you understand. If a particular point is unclear to you, ask a question to clarify it before you respond.

Even if you think you understand the message, make sure you do by clarifying it with the your spouse.. You might say something like:

- "Just to be sure I understand you, let me repeat back to you what I thought you said…"

- "I heard you say… Is that correct?"

- "If I understand correctly, your concern is…"

Pride can destroy a marriage quickly. Never forget that marriage is for the humble! There are going to be many times in your marriage that you have to sacrifice what you want or need for the sake of your spouse. There are going to be times when you will have to serve them in ways you've never had to serve anyone else. NEVER see yourself as so big or great that you cannot meet any need for your spouse. The second pride sneaks in in that way, love begins to erode at the seams.

Part of being humble is being a good listener. After all, communication is vital to our marriages! You can't be a good communicator without being a good listener. After all, how are you going to know the needs and desires of your spouse if you aren't taking the time to listen to and invest in them in the first place?

Being a bad listener, or not taking the time to listen at all, can cause emotional distance in your marriage. This emotional distance erodes the unity in your marriage, and you begin to seek what's best for you instead of what's best for your partner. Take the time daily to listen to your spouse, genuinely investing in the events of their day and the emotions they are feeling. Create an environment within your marriage where your spouse knows they can always freely talk with you about anything and that you will have an ear to lend.

You and your spouse can talk without communicating. Communication goes deeper than mere talking. You speak with a lot of people, but you truly communicate with those closest to you. Communication comprises our choice of words, tone, and facial expressions. All of these aspects come together to show the other person that you care. When speaking with your spouse, consider both what you say and HOW you say it. When you invest in your spouse's goals, dreams, and feelings, it shows by how you communicate with them. Authentic communication shows your husband/wife that you are invested in them.

Pride can lead to disagreements and heated conversation. There may come times when you and your spouse disagree, but there is NEVER a valid reason to be disrespectful. Speaking to your spouse in this way crushes their heart, erodes trust, and creates distance between you. Not only that but broken trust and hurt feelings take a very long time to heal. Commit to always treating your spouse with respect, even when working through a disagreement. Speak words of empowerment to your husband/wife in all situations, and you will be amazed by the growth in your marriage.

Tips for Effective Listening

- Most of us are distracted, preoccupied or forgetful about 75% of the time we should be listening.

- We listen at 125-250 words per minute, but think at 1000-3000 words per minute.

- Immediately after we listen to someone, we only recall about 50% of what they said.

- Long-term, we only remember 20% of what we hear.

- More than 35 business studies indicate that listening is a top skill needed for success in business.

Reflection Questions:

1. How is the current state of communication within your marriage? How is it affecting your relationship, for better or worse?

2. No matter where you find your level of communication currently, how can you make it even better? What steps do you need to take to catapult your marriage to the next level?

Action Tips:

➤ Make quality time for one another EVERY DAY. A lot or a little time is less important than making sure that you are spending QUALITY time together. That means no phones, and no distractions: it's time for you and your spouse to talk, catch up, and simply enjoy being with one another.

➤ Commit to speaking words of love and encouragement into the life of your spouse daily. Find a fun practice to engage in to accomplish this. Perhaps you leave a loving note in your spouse's lunch that you know they will see at work; maybe you decide to tell them something you love or admire about them each day; or maybe you just want to start simply making sure to say, "I love you" every day!

Scriptures for Prayer and Reflection:

James 1:19: *"My dear brothers and sisters, take note of this: Everyone should be quick to listen, slow to speak and slow to become angry."*

Proverbs 15:1: *"A gentle answer deflects anger, but harsh words make tempers flare."*

Proverbs 18:2: *"Fools have no interest in understanding; they only want to air their own opinions."*

Colossians 3:8: *"But now is the time to get rid of anger, rage, malicious behavior, slander, and dirty language."*

Prayer

Lord, we know that communication is vital to our relationship. Guide us into developing the communication between us. Help us to talk to one another with open and vulnerable hearts always. We long for the peace, love, and intimacy that stem from a marriage abounding in solid communication. Amen.

CHAPTER 6:

The 4 Types of Intimacy

"Spiritual friendship is eagerly helping one another know, serve, love, and resemble God in deeper and deeper ways."

-Tim Keller-

Intimacy is integral to a healthy marriage. Without it, spouses drift apart, conflict arises, and marriages crumble. While the word is often used to talk about sex, intimacy is about so much more! In this chapter, we are going to talk about the four types of intimacy, how they help to strengthen our marriages, and some tips on how to work on each in your marriage.

Before you can work on intimacy in marriage, it's important to understand the four main types: emotional, intellectual, sexual, and experiential intimacy. Let's explore these in terms of how they apply to a romantic relationship.

Emotional Intimacy

People experience emotional intimacy when they feel comfortable sharing their feelings—good and bad—with each other. For example, you tell your spouse that you feel insecure about your body after gaining a few pounds. This is not information you'd share with anyone. You are being open with your feelings in a way that leaves you vulnerable. To do this with someone, you have to have a certain level of love and trust between you, something essential to have within your marriage.

Emotional intimacy is one of the crucial building blocks of a thriving marriage. If you can't share your feelings with your spouse, something is wrong. There should be no none you feel closer to and more comfortable sharing your feelings with than your spouse.

While it may come easy to you, emotional intimacy can be challenging for many people! Because of the trauma of past abusive relationships, many people can put up walls around themselves, even in marriage. They won't let anyone, even their spouse, fully into their emotional space. This is challenging but a very real struggle that many people face.

It's crucial that we find healthy ways to process our past hurts and pain so that we don't find ourselves in this situation. No matter what we've been through, we cannot be emotionally distant from our spouses. Doing so will only serve to cause to suffocate our marriages and cause further hurt in our lives.

This is not to downplay the very real and traumatizing pain many of us have felt in relationships in the past. You don't have to simply forget what you've been through and stuff the pain away. But there are steps to take to process and heal from that pain. There's no shame in even seeking help from a professionally trained Christian counselor to help you through the process. You owe it to yourself, your spouse, and your marriage to come to the point in your life where you can open up to your spouse again.

As hard as it is, allow your spouse to become part of that healing process. Walking through that pain together and seeking healing from it is exactly the kind of emotional intimacy that can take your marriage to the next level. Going through an experience like that together will make you closer than ever before.

Intellectual Intimacy

When it comes to intellectual intimacy, people feel safe sharing their ideas and opinions, even when they don't see eye to eye on the matter. For example, you and your spouse discuss your personal political opinions, even though you follow different parties. This is a wonderfully healthy thing to do! It shows that you care about your spouse by fully listening to their opinions, that you respect them by allowing them to hold those opinions without conflict, and that you trust them enough to share your own without fear of judgment.

Sadly, many couples have not learned to do this. Early in their relationship, many people don't talk about hot-button topics like religion, politics, plans for the future, etc. They are having so much fun in their relationship that the early spark of chemistry between them blinds them from the need to share their thoughts and opinions on certain topics with one another.

Some people will make it all the way to marriage either neglecting to ever speak of their opinions on certain things or outright ignoring the topics. But they eventually come up, causing conflict later on. By time they do get around to sharing intellectual intimacy, they are so surprised by what they are hearing that they can lash out in response to their spouse's differing opinions.

We must be very careful in how we respond to our spouse when they share their thoughts and feelings with us. We must NEVER marginalize or disregard their opinions. If we do, we are not only closing off our relationship to further intellectual intimacy, but we are cutting our marriage off to emotional intimacy as well. We will only hurt our spouse, causing a breach of trust which will make them feel uncomfortable in sharing their thoughts and feelings in the future.

Sexual Intimacy

Sexual intimacy occurs when people engage in sensual or sexual activities. For example, your spouse pulls you in close, lifts your chin, and kisses you passionately. This type of intimacy is about so much more than sex itself. We must remember the sacredness and intimacy of all the physical expressions we experience in marriage so that we can recapture what true sexual intimacy is all about.

For instance, some people will have sex with a complete stranger. It is purely physical, and no intimacy is shared there. That's because so much more feeds into TRUE sexual intimacy! For your sexual intimacy in marriage to truly transform your marriage, you and your spouse must capture not only the physical aspect but also the mental, emotional, and spiritual parts of it as well.

When sexual intimacy is expressed within a godly relationship that's intimate on every level, amazing things happen. It becomes an act that builds security, closeness, and trust between spouses in a beautiful and holy way. Sex then transcends being a physical act and brings the couple closer to each other, and to God, in new and exciting ways.

Experiential Intimacy

People engage in experiential intimacy when they bond during day-to-day activities or work together to accomplish a mission. For example, you help your spouse to fix the flat tire on your car, handing her the tools she needs. As you learn and develop these skills together, you grow closer!

You can be intentional in growing together in experiential intimacy. Seek out opportunities to experience new things together or learn new skills as a team. Do an improvement project on your house/apartment together; take a painting class with your spouse; or take an online course together on a subject you're mutually interested in. These are endless opportunities to be found for you and your significant other to learn and grow together.

There will also be opportunities that naturally arise as you go through life together. The next time something breaks or needs fixing at home, make time to tackle it together! The next time the kids need help with their homework, try working through it as a team! Yes, there are times where it's appropriate and necessary to do things on our own, but it shouldn't always be that way. Setting aside time to tackle some of these things together can give your marriage a HUGE boost of intimacy!

Top Issues Arising from Intimacy Concerns

Not Getting Enough Sex

It's important that we are willing to give of ourselves physically for our partner. Even the Bible speaks to this! **1 Corinthians 7:5** reads, "*Do not deprive each other of sexual relations, unless you both agree to refrain from sexual intimacy for a limited time so you can give yourselves more completely to prayer.*"

Why would the Bible take the time to encourage married couples to make sure they are not depriving each other of sex? Because it's important for our marriages! Of course, there are times and places where we must ask our partners to wait for sex. But, in general, if we are healthy and able, we should not be denying our spouse physical intimacy over an extended period of time.

When this happens, trust and intimacy are eroded. Also, the spouse being denied may start to experience feelings of self-doubt, asking themselves questions like: "Is something wrong with me? Does my spouse still find me attractive? Are they cheating on me? These kinds of doubts can crush your spouse's self-esteem. And we're here to build up our spouses, not tear them down!

Have open and honest communication between you and your spouse over expectations on sex. How often do you feel that need? How can you support the other person in what they're going through so they're ready body, heart, and mind to engage in that kind of intimacy? These are the kinds of questions you should ask. Make sure you're being the best listener you can be and commit to following through on helping to meet the needs of your spouse as they express them to you.

Not Prioritizing Sex in the Relationship

More often than not, a lack of sex in marriage doesn't come from spouses feeling unattracted or out of love with one another, but rather from exhaustion and busyness! Many of us, at the end of a long time, just don't have the time, energy, and aren't in the right state of mind for sex. That is not necessarily something either you or your spouse are doing wrong, but just a product of the kind of lifestyles we live that we need to be aware of.

We live in a world of never-ending responsibilities and demands on our time. Yet, in the midst of it, we have to prioritize intimacy with our partner. No matter how much work needs to be done or how many bills need to be paid, at the end of the day those things are NOT more important than your marriage! Even though it seems impossible sometimes, you CAN prioritize more efficiently and make time for your spouse.

Sit down with your spouse, making a list of all the things you want and need to do on a daily basis. Work through each item on that list one by one, asking each other the following questions:

1. Is this something I NEED to do?

2. Is this too high on my list of priorities?

3. Is this task holding me back from accomplishing something else more important?

4. Do I need to move this priority up or down on my list, or perhaps remove it entirely?

This can be a tedious, challenging, and sometimes painful process. But I assure you, it's SO WORTH IT! Once you have your priorities in place, it will eliminate so much stress in your life for both you and your spouse. And in the midst of it, you'll find yourself with more and more opportunities of free time to spend with your spouse, deepening your relationship through sharing intimacy.

Not Communicating When There's an Issue

There's no avoiding trouble in this life, no matter how hard we try. Having a successful marriage is not about avoiding trials in life, but rather about how you process and work through them TOGETHER. The absolute worst thing you can do is not communicate with your spouse when an issue arises.

When you avoid communicating over an issue, it breaks many kinds of intimacy. Emotional intimacy is stunted because you aren't being open in honestly sharing the issue with your spouse. Intellectual intimacy is lost because you aren't sharing your thoughts on the issue with your spouse. Your sexual intimacy is held back from its full potential because there are unspoken things between you and your spouse. On top of it all, you lose a powerful opportunity to experience experiential intimacy by casting aside the opportunity to work through the problem and figure it out together.

The Truth About Sex

God thinks sex is awesome. So awesome that He decided to make it the only way that we bring new life into this world. No matter how much we may try to avoid the topic sometimes or treat it as taboo, there is no denying that how we view sex is critical to experiencing healthy intimacy in our marriages.

Let's talk about what the Bible says the truth about sex is. Sex is an expression of the oneness in marriage: *"and the two are united into one.' Since they are no longer two but one"* (Mark 10:8). It is two people, who have made a life-long commitment to one another, expressing the image of God together and reflecting it more clearly. Think about it. Men and women are both different, but both have the image of God within them. What happens when they join as one? They reflect that image more fully! Sex in marriage is a physical expression of this truth. We find power in living out truth in a physical way. That's what we do in worship. We are acting out our faith in a physical way, praising God with our bodies. Isn't sex the same way? So, think of it as an act of worship to God, when it's done in the confines of marriage according to God's plan.

In contrast to this, the world promotes sex as a pleasure, something we can indulge in with whoever we want. Millions of TV shows, movies, magazines, etc. promote it as far, far less than what it truly is. This is what our youth is seeing and what is shaping their perception of sex. They are being robbed of seeing the true value, the true fulfillment, and the true significance that it holds. That's why so many grow up ending up very hurt in their relationships and struggling to ever find lasting happiness in love.

What God wants them to find in sex is lifelong love, security, and fulfillment. God wants to shape our minds to see sex as a complete giving of oneself to their spouse, and the receiving of the other in return. It is a beautiful way to say, "I give myself up to live for you" while your spouse says the same. It can serve as a reminder of how to live this out in our everyday lives as well, putting the needs of your spouse before you own. That's why the Bible says, *"Do not deprive each other of sexual relations"* (1 Corinthians 7:5). It's a gentle nudge to focus on the needs of your spouse before your own. It is a reminder to continually return to the love that sparked your relationship in the first place. It helps us never to forget that sex is not only an act of receiving but also of giving. This mutual giving and receiving serves to strengthen our bonds with our spouse.

I challenge you to ask God to reshape the way that you view sex and help to teach you how to express it. Let us together remind the world of the true value that it holds, instead of diminishing its worth so greatly.

In marriage, God has called us to be righteous, holy, and pure. There is no place for sin or anything improper in our love. We are to live out our marriages against the standard of God's Word just as we would in any other area of our lives.

God has a special design for sex in marriage. To understand further god's design for sex within marriage, a large area of conflict for couples, we must first look at the definition for the word "sacrament:" an outward expression of an inward reality. Think about this for a moment, and it makes so much sense. Baptism is a physical act that is an outward expression of the inner change that's happening within us as we devote ourselves to Christ and his church. The eucharist is a physical expression of our communion with Christ and the acceptance of his body and blood for our salvation.

So, how does this relate to god's design for sex within marriage? Sex, in god's eyes, is a physical act that is an outward expression of the inward reality of the unity of husband and wife. We are one flesh in marriage. God has taken two and made them one. Two people bearing his image come together in a profound act of love. How beautiful and meaningful is that? Doesn't it change the way you view sex in marriage?

John McArthur says it perfectly: *"according to the bible, the marriage act is more than a physical act. It is an act of sharing. It is an act of communion. It is an act of total self-giving wherein the husband gives himself completely to the wife, and the wife gives herself to the husband in such a way that the two actually become one flesh."*

Let this newfound perspective on what sex is really all about quell any conflict that arises in your marriage that has to do with your sexual relationship. Sex is a gift from God. He designed it to be an act that brings the married couple to a level of intimacy achieved nowhere else. Sex is holy, and a sexless relationship is a big warning sign that your marriage is in a bad place. Even when life gets busy, find ways to keep your sex life thriving. Let your intimacy be a place that promotes love, security, and healing. There you will find a oneness with your spouse that will propel you to a healthier marriage.

Genesis 2:24 says, *"Therefore a man shall leave his father and his mother and hold fast to his wife, and they shall become one flesh."* In the eyes of many, the value of marriage is falling fast. Society is rejecting more and more the biblical ideal for marriage. Let's face it: many of us have seen it fail firsthand.

We need strong couples to rise up and demonstrate why marriage still matters. The world needs to see God at work through the union of two people that He has called together for a purpose. Relying on God's strength, a new generation of husbands and wives can represent Christ in the unique way that only they can. You, as a couple, can be part of this revolution in how marriage is viewed in our society today.

Men and women are different, but both bear the image of God within them. That means there is something about both men's and women's distinctive qualities that express something about God.

Marriage is an act of worship because when that couple lives out their relationship in unity, they form a more complete reflection of God's image in humanity. Marriage is holy. **Matthew 19:6** reads, *"What God has joined together, let no one separate."* If God has brought the married couple together, their marriage is an honorable and valuable union.

Men and women were made for each other, both reflecting the image of God in their unique way. When they come together in the way God intended, He shares with them the power to do what previously only He could do: bring forth life.

Marriage Builds Healthy Families

As children, our very first relationship is with our parents. Our bond with them and understanding of family is one of the first places we form our identity. The family unit's health is critical to the development of the children born into that family. Through a loving marriage, parents empower and reflect God's love for their child. A powerful, impactful marriage is the best thing that we can give our children.

A revitalization of marriage could strongly influence the world for God's Kingdom. It all starts with us. The way we understand and live out God's intentions for marriage, the better witnesses we will be for the Gospel. Marriage is the foundation for healthy, godly families. The children born from those families will become our future.

Seek God Together

The spiritual wellness of your relationship will go a long way in determining your marriage's success. Do you and your spouse have a similar core value system? Are you united in Christ together? Do you help one another become a better child of God? The answers to these questions will help you evaluate the places you need to focus on in your marriage. Always strive for unity in belief, faith, and practice. If you are not on the same path, how can you walk together? When you seek God as a couple, you will surely find Him. He will lead you exactly where you need to be.

Don't settle for anything less than the vibrant, fulfilling marriage that God has called you to experience. Commit to growing with your spouse daily while striving to keep these five steps to building a healthy marriage as the foundation of your relationship. There is a reason that God brought you and your spouse together in the first place. Do not let that purpose pass you by. You can capture it together while building a healthy marriage that will last a lifetime. Your key to doing this is to develop strong intimacy in every way!

Reflection Questions

1. How did reading about the four types of intimacy open your eyes to the ways you connect with your spouse?

2. Consider God's design for sex in marriage. Does it match up with the personal beliefs you've held? If not, how can you bring your feelings into alignment with God's design?

Action Tips

➢ Discuss the four types of intimacy with your spouse. In which of these areas do you thrive? Which need more effort or care? Strategize together on how you can achieve better intimacy in every way, taking turns and patiently listening to your partner's needs.

➢ Discuss with your spouse the ways in which you seek God together. How is that process going? Make goals to become closer to God as a couple.

Scriptures for Prayer and Meditation

Matthew 19:6: *"What God has joined together, let no one separate."*

Genesis 2:24: *"Therefore a man shall leave his father and his mother and hold fast to his wife, and they shall become one flesh."*

1 Corinthians 7:5: "*Do not deprive each other of sexual relations, unless you both agree to refrain from sexual intimacy for a limited time so you can give yourselves more completely to prayer.*"

Prayer

Lord, thank You for the way intimacy in all its forms shapes our marriage. Show us how intimacy is to be expressed and how it can draw us closer together than ever before. Our love is important, and we wish to learn how to express it according to Your design. Amen.

CHAPTER 7:

Managing Expectations

"You often hear it said that people have bad marriages, but in fact, this is not true. Marriage is a God instituted covenant between a man and a woman, and it is good. That has never changed. The institution hasn't failed – people are failing to work out their problems. Couples are simply giving up and walking away, or simply have no idea what they can try next. The good news is that even "soured" relationships can be healed. Things can change. People can change. Marriages can be better than they ever were before."

-Karen M. Gray-

We can't tell you how many young couples we've spoken with who get married without discussing essential expectations first. Then, after they have married, they come back to us in shock and sadness that they are not on the same page with their spouse!

When you are young and in love, the word "expectations" is not something that's typically at the forefront of your mind. You are madly in love with you your spouse or spouse-to-be, and you figure that living together will be bliss. But while living with and doing life alongside another person, things get real very quickly. You get to know that person better than ever before, inside and out. Part of that is learning the intimate details of their wants and needs in any given situation. Here is where our expectations come into play.

Who do you expect to handle the bills? How often do you expect to have sex? How much time does each person expect to spend doing their own thing, and how much time do you expect to spend with one another? How about seeing family on the holidays? How does each of you feel about boundaries in your home?

These are all questions that are going to come up within your marriage. It would serve you well to speak on these things beforehand so that you aren't blindsided by them when they arrive (the expectations I mean, not the in-laws!)

These expectations don't have to diminish the intense love you have for one another. Living with one another can still be bliss! But it takes some thought and preparation beforehand, just like anything else worth striving for. You can't go into it without truly and deeply investing in one another to the point where you are prepared to meet the other's unique needs in the way that will serve them best.

Biblical Example: When Expectations are Broken

Hosea's love story and marriage with Gomer is an example of forgiveness and compassion when expectations are broken. Despite sin, deceit, and broken trust, people can restore their relationships with God's love and guidance.

Now, in marriage, a non-negotiable and obvious expectation is that both partners will remain faithful to one another, right? In the book of Hosea, we meet Hosea and Gomer. Hosea was instructed by God to marry Gomer, who turned out to be a promiscuous woman. Eventually, Gomer committed adultery, leaving Hosea heartbroken. One of the biggest and most crucial marriage expectations was not held, and as you can imagine, it left Hosea feeling lost and hurt.

Hosea had every right and reason to divorce Gomer on the spot. While the Bible doesn't condone divorce, it does make the one exception of marital unfaithfulness. But Hosea decides to walk in the way of the Lord and show extraordinary love, grace, and mercy. Hosea takes Gomer back into his life with renewed trust and forgiveness. This story tells us that even when expectations are broken in a relationship and conflict ensues, with forgiveness and love, restoration is possible.

God, the Ultimate Provider of all our Needs

This message of forgiveness, love, and grace is so important because no matter how much you love your spouse, they aren't perfect! They will let you down at some point, as you will to them. It may not be as extreme as the case with Hosea and Gomer (at least I hope not!), but it will still happen, nonetheless.

In these times, forgiveness can be hard, I get it. But you must practice forgiveness, nonetheless. Show your spouse the love and mercy that Christ has shown to you. And while you are forgiving them, remember that God is ultimately the provider of all of your needs. He can bring you fulfillment, happiness, and peace in a way that even your spouse never could. That's why your relationship must involve Him. You and your spouse will meet each other's needs but ultimately rely on God for true and lasting satisfaction.

The Bible assures us that we can trust in God to take care of us in every way imaginable. **Philippians 4:19** says, *"God will meet all your needs according to the riches of his glory in Christ Jesus."* Notice the wording here? ALL your needs. Not SOME of your needs, but ALL of them.

God loves to take care of His children, and you can trust that He will do so for you and your spouse.

A worldview shift is essential. **Matthew 6:33** says, "*Seek first his kingdom and his righteousness, and all these things will be given to you as well.*" If we keep our eyes focused on God's Kingdom and the eternity that He is leading us to, the conflicts that arise in our marriage will seem that much smaller and when our expectations are broken, they will be that much easier to forgive.

Reflection Questions:

1. Why are expectations important? Have you spoken about expectations in your relationship?

2. How are we to respond when expectations are broken in marriage? When we respond as Christ would, how does it bring immense healing to our marriage?

Action Tips:

> ➢ If you haven't already, through prayer, sit down with your spouse and make a list of healthy and godly expectations for your marriage. Make sure they are mutual and created through a posture of prayer. Commit to holding one another accountable for these expectations.

Scripture for Prayer and Reflection:

Hebrews 13:4: *"Give honor to marriage, and remain faithful to one another in marriage. God will surely judge people who are immoral and those who commit adultery."*

Ephesians 4:2-3: *"Always be humble and gentle. Be patient with each other, making allowance for each other's faults because of your love. Make every effort to keep yourselves united in the Spirit, binding yourselves together with peace."*

Prayer

Lord, come into our marriage and help us to manage expectations in a healthy way. Teach us how to be open and honest with one another about our wants and needs without judgment. As we do, fill us with patience, love, and gentleness toward one another. Amen.

CHAPTER 8:

Navigating Finances

"Money may be an inanimate object, but we attach great emotional significance to it. Money only becomes our friend if we as a couple learn to partner around the decisions related to money. One of the prerequisites for partnering in the matter of money is an understanding of the meaning of money to each of us."

-Dr. David Stoop and Dr Jan Stoop-

The next story is one that may be more common than you would think. We knew a couple, Ashley and Derek, that was thriving in every way. Many of us who knew them were honestly inspired by their love for one another and faith in God. They were a couple we would have told people to model their own marriages after. But there was something secret going on behind the scenes that led to a major conflict in their relationship.

The one thing they weren't on the same page about was money. It wasn't that they were at odds on the topic, but rather that they never really discussed it in the first place. Neither partner knew how the other was spending and never asked about it.

After years of this kind of lifestyle, it got them into some deep waters financially. Both were caught off guard by the situation and it led to conflict between them as they tried to navigate their way through it.

Thankfully, they weathered the storm and learned a lot from the experience. Needless to say, they did things much differently and more responsibly going forward!

Sadly, finances are one of the top reasons statistically for divorce. It's a tragic and harrowing truth of our world, but it doesn't have to be that way. It's only like that because so many people find themselves woefully unprepared to navigate their finances when they enter marriage with one another!

You'd be amazed how even a little bit of budgeting, preparation, and planning can completely change how you navigate your finances in marriage. It's an essential topic to discuss with your partner, no matter if it's something that you're naturally keen on or enjoy talking about. It doesn't have to be an everyday discussion, but the proper expectations and planning are needed for success.

Make it an exercise that you do together as a couple. Bond over it. Make goals together. It's a wonderful way to celebrate what you are accomplishing as a couple and to envision your goals for your future together.

What the Bible Says

While money is important and it's good to be responsible, we must never let it become an idol in our lives. So many people have stumbled into this pitfall, and that becomes a whole other problem itself. Hebrews 13:5 says, *"Don't love money; be satisfied with what you have. For God has said, "I will never fail you. I will never abandon you."*

As a couple, it's essential that you ultimately trust in God to provide all of your needs. If you handle your finances responsibly and work together for the betterment of your future, you can trust God to take care of the rest. If you follow Him, He will always walk right alongside you, guiding you precisely where He wants you to go. You can trust that that will be a place of prosperity and abundance for you because God desires nothing but the best for His children.

Tithing

Tithing is a crucial exercise in God's provisions when placing your trust in Him. Tithing says that you trust God to provide for you and that you want to invest in the furtherance of the Gospel. The ministries of the church are able to function on your support, and those who devote their life to the Lord vocationally make ends meet by the resources that you provide. It's a beautiful thing to tithe, and God will bless you greatly for it! Proverbs 3:9-10 says, *"Honor the* LORD *with your wealth and with the best part of everything you produce. Then he will fill your barns with grain, and your vats will overflow with good wine."*

It's crucial that you and your spouse are aligned on tithing. To be on the same page in tithing means having a unified understanding of using your resources to further the cause of the Gospel as a couple. This is vital as God as called each of us to be stewards of the money He has entrusted us with. Part of being a good steward is giving back to further the mission of the church.

While it may feel strange to consider giving money away as prospering as a couple/family, God's definition of what it means to prosper is different than that of the world. To the world, prospering means hoarding money at all costs, even when it negatively affects others. God's definition of prospering financially is providing for ourselves and our family while also realizing that our financial security is a gift from God. To honor Him, we need to give back to the causes that are important to Him.

Set Healthy Financial Goals

On top of budgeting together, also make healthy financial goals with your spouse. Ask each other questions like, "What do we want to have saved in five years? Ten? What are we saving for? How can we best use our resources to honor God?"

When you base your financial goals on questions like this, you will have a focused path forward. Make your goals attainable, and set regular times to check-in together. During those check-in times, see how things are progressing and if any tweaks need to be made to your goals.

Reflection Questions

1. Why is it essential to plan, prepare, and budget finances in your marriage? Why is it something that you can't simply ignore in your marriage?

2. Why is tithing important? How does God bless us when we tithe?

Action Tips

- ➢ If you haven't already, make time to sit down and create a budget with your spouse. If you have, revisit that budget and revise it accordingly.

- ➢ Schedule a regular time to sit together and do a "check-up" on your budget and tighten up your plans and financial goals for the future.

- ➢ Through prayer, discuss together how God desires that you would use your benefits to bless the church and fuel its mission. Commit to following God together wherever it is that He may lead.

Scripture for Prayer and Reflection:

Hebrews 13:5: *"Don't love money; be satisfied with what you have. For God has said, "I will never fail you. I will never abandon you."*

1 Timothy 6:17-19: *"Teach those who are rich in this world not to be proud and not to trust in their money, which is so unreliable. Their trust should be in God, who richly gives us all we need for our enjoyment. Tell them to use their money to do good. They should be rich in good works and generous to those in need, always being ready to share with others. By doing this they will be storing up their treasure as a good foundation for the future so that they may experience true life."*

Proverbs 3:9-10: "*Honor the* LORD *with your wealth and with the best part of everything you produce. Then he will fill your barns with grain, and your vats will overflow with good wine.*"

Prayer

Lord, thank You for the opportunity to create and enjoy financial security in this life. Help us to manage our finances responsibly and in a way that honors the stewardship You have entrusted us with. We desire to use our finances to further Your purposes in the world. Amen.

CHAPTER 9:

The Spiritual Reality of Marriage

"God compared the church to a marriage. Until the church realizes the covenant of spouses is vital for the health of the church, the community, it will continue to decline in relevance."

-Aaron Behr-

We knew a couple who had lived together forever before finally deciding to get married. They saw marriage as a legal contract and something unimportant. After all, what was the government's recognition of their relationship to them if they were already happy and in love?

But the time came when Marilyn realized that there was something deeper missing from their life. As they became older and the pressures of life mounted, she suddenly understood that there was much more to marriage than what they were experiencing. Maybe God did have a role to play in it all after all and it was time to invite Him in and get married for real.

But Adam was not so keen on the idea. He was rooted in the life they had built together and was opposed to change. His eyes were blinded to the truth that Marilyn so desperately wanted for him to see. Because of it, conflict arose between them that kept them from the deep and resounding spiritual reality of marriage.

Sadly, this happens quite often and it's heartbreaking. God made marriage to be so much more than anything we could ever imagine! We must understand and embrace the spiritual reality of God's design for marriage so that we can experience its fullness together.

God's Holy Design for Marriage

Ephesians 5:21-32 says: *And further, submit to one another out of reverence for Christ. For wives, this means submit to your husbands as to the Lord. For a husband is the head of his wife as Christ is the head of the church. He is the Savior of his body, the church. As the church submits to Christ, so you wives should submit to your husbands in everything. For husbands, this means love your wives, just as Christ loved the church. He gave up his life for her to make her holy and clean, washed by the cleansing of God's word. He did this to present her to himself as a glorious church without a spot or wrinkle or any other blemish. Instead, she will be holy and without fault. In the same way, husbands ought to love their wives as they love their own bodies. For a man who loves his wife actually shows love for himself. No one hates his own body but feeds and cares for it, just as Christ cares for the church. And we are members of his body. As the Scriptures say, "A man leaves his father and mother and is joined to his wife, and the two are united into one." This is a great mystery, but it is an illustration of the way Christ and the church are one.*

This is a famous biblical passage on marriage. There is so much to unpack here regarding the beautiful and holy mystery that God has created marriage to be!

First off, Paul encourages us to submit to one another out of reverence for Christ. What does this mean? It means that we seek to meet the needs of our spouse before our own. It means that we show the same kind of love that Christ displayed to others throughout His life to our spouse. That doesn't mean we neglect our own needs. When both spouses are committed to this way of life, both spouses' needs are met!

There's a beautiful truth to be found early on in the bible. **Genesis 2:24** says, *"Therefore a man shall leave his father and his mother and hold fast to his wife, and they shall become one flesh."* This one flesh that we become refers to the mysterious, beautiful, and incomparable unity that we experience as husband and wife.

This unity is built upon the foundations of love and respect that Paul mentions in Ephesians 5. The wife is called to respect the husband and his unique role in the relationship, while the husband is called to do what? Love his wife as Christ loved the church! And did Christ do for the church? He gave everything, including his very life. This is the foundation of our faith, and it is also the foundation of our marriages.

To end the passage, Paul affirms this beautiful full circle that we come to. He claims that the unity we live out in marriage is a reflection of the unity of Christ and the church. How beautiful is that? Doesn't it completely change the way that you view marriage?

John C. Broger sums up the meaning of this passage perfectly: *"God intends and expects marriage to be a lifetime commitment between a man and a woman, based on the principles of biblical love. The relationship between Jesus Christ and his church is the supreme example of the committed love that a husband and wife are to follow in their relationship with each other."*

Oneness

Oneness is complete unity with each other- spirit, soul, and body. The oneness God has intended us to experience in marriage is completely unlike anything we could ever experience with anyone else.

In **Matthew 19:1-5**, Jesus is questioned about marriage and divorce:

"When Jesus had finished saying these things, he left Galilee and went into the region of Judea to the other side of the Jordan. Large crowds followed him, and he healed them there.

Some Pharisees came to him to test him. They asked, "Is it lawful for a man to divorce his wife for any and every reason?"

"Haven't you read," he replied, "that at the beginning the Creator 'made them male and female,' and said, 'For this reason a man will leave his

father and mother and be united to his wife, and the two will become one flesh'? So they are no longer two, but one flesh. Therefore what God has joined together, let no one separate."

Jesus doesn't mince words here. Jesus knows God's perfect design for marriage and wanted to relay that message strongly. He says quite clearly that husband and wife will become ONE flesh. Then, just to drive it home even further, He emphasizes that they are no longer, two, but ONE. This is the basis of our understanding of oneness in marriage, body, mind, and spirit.

But what does that actually mean? It means that we love, care for, and give to our spouse as we would for ourselves, even putting their needs above our own. We give to them physically, mentally, spiritually, and emotionally with all love, vulnerability, respect, and compassion. We hold nothing back from the, giving of ourselves in such an open way that it's terrifying, but those fears are quickly quelled in the arms of our spouse who accepts us and love us just as we are.

Oneness in marriage is all about joining your lives together so securely in every way that you operate as one in mission, love, and family. United together, under the Lord, you have power, strength, and love. God made you and your spouse differently, since you are both individuals, male and female. But the Bible tells us that God made both men and women in His image: So *"God created mankind in his own image, in the image of God he created them; male and female he created them"* (**Genesis 1:27**).

This means that something about both you and your spouse, your nature as male and female, and being different individuals, reflects something unique of God. We all reflect something beautiful about God like a mirror, for we were created in His image from an overflow of His love. But when we join as one with our spouse, a clearer picture is presented, and we reflect God even more brilliantly.

Marriage is Merger and not Acquisition

When you consider the world of business, you see a couple different things happen sometimes between two businesses. Sometimes, companies merge, joining forces together to make both stronger. Other times, one company completely absorbs the other who was struggling and needed to sell their assets.

This analogy can help in our mindset toward marriage. In your mind, is your spouse something you acquired that adds to your life? Or, have your lives merged, creating a new, stronger entity together? Marriage is a merger, NOT an acquisition!

If we treat marriage like an acquisition, we will encounter much conflict in our relationship.

If we treat marriage as a merger, we will stand strong and united together, even in the face of conflict.

You can't give yourself an out: your flesh will take it every time. "Divorce" shouldn't be a word that's even in your vocabulary. In the darkest moments of your marriage, you can't even give yourself the option of giving up. Our flesh is weak, and we will be compelled to take that escape every time! But it's not worth it. You need to fight for your marriage at all costs. You need to make the commitment to be by your spouse's side throughout everything you experience together.

Sadly, most people experience a performance-based relationship in most marriages. We naturally have expectations of our spouses in our marriages. This is healthy and creates important boundaries. But our spouses are also human. There will come times when they become exhausted, overwhelmed, and in need of extra support.

In these times, they may not fulfill all of the expectations we have for them in our marriage. This can create challenges for many couples. One spouse has to carry extra weight for a season and carry resentment toward their spouse with them as a result.

When we are faced with this kind of situation, we have a choice to make. We can either:

1. Partner with our spouse, supporting them in their time of trials and helping them to pull through it, or:

2. Bear the extra weight with resentment, not feeding into our spouse and letting them figure things out on their own.

I'm sure you don't have to guess what the healthiest choice for your relationship is. Remember, true love means loving, supporting, and taking care of your spouse, even when they aren't at their best. Your spouse should NEVER have to continually and consistently perform to "earn" your love. Your love should always be there for them unconditionally.

Nothing reveals selflessness more than marriage. In marriage, we aren't there to love our spouse only when it's easy: we must love them and care for them in every season. Sometimes, that will involve heavy self-sacrifice. But rest assured that anything you do for the betterment or care of your spouse is SO WORTH IT. Through every situation you experience together, God will bring you closer and help to develop selfless character within you.

Ephesians 5:29-33 *says,* "*No one abuses his own body, does he? No, he feeds and pampers it. That's how Christ treats us, the church, since we are part of his body. And this is why a man leaves father and mother and cherishes his wife. No* *longer two, they become "one flesh." This is a huge mystery, and I don't pretend to understand it all. What is clearest to me is the way Christ treats the church. And this provides a good picture of how each husband is to treat his wife, loving himself in loving her, and how each wife is to honor her husband."*

We will all go through seasons of marriage. There is a difference between abuse and a tough season. Abuse is NEVER acceptable. We cannot cover-up abuse by making excuses for our spouse and simply calling it a tough season. While every relationship does eb and flow, hitting its own highs and lows, there are ALWAYS healthy boundaries that must be maintained in how we are to treat one another.

Marriage as Covenant

In non-biblical terms, a covenant is essentially a legal, binding agreement. When you get married, take out a loan, lease a house, or sign a document, you are entering into a type of covenant: an agreement in which both parties make certain promises to one another.

In biblical terms, a covenant between God and people holds great significance and forms the foundation of how God interacts with people. When we approach marriage as a covenant, we are truly making a lifelong commitment, a joining and binding contract that cannot be broken, and only grows stronger and more meaningful with time.

Marriage as a covenant is different than other types of contracts that we form in life because it is forever and cannot be broken. Look at these powerful words from Jesus that show just how permanent a marriage covenant is: *"For example, a man who divorces his wife and marries someone else commits adultery. And anyone who marries a woman divorced from her husband commits adultery"* (**Luke 16:18**). Jesus is trying to make it clear that even if you separate and get a divorce in the eyes of society, in the eyes of God you are still in a marriage covenant with your spouse.

This is not meant to be restrictive, binding, or cruel. This covenant relationship fosters real love, lasting love, and strong families. It's a kind of relationship that persists through the pressures and burdens of life, blooming more and more despite what's happening around it, because it is rooted in the Lord. The foundation of the marriage covenant is in God's love, a love that is mightier than any trial that we face in this life.

Popular media presents love in such a twisted, ungodly way. There's so much passion but so little commitment. Watch any romantic movie and you'll see it. Typically one, if not both, of the characters involved start in a relationship with someone else, sometimes even a marriage. Then, the two characters meet, and the passion between them is undeniable. This leads them on a long and dramatic journey toward one another, eventually ending up together and leaving their other partners behind.

This is a shameful image for what marriage and true love are all about. God has designed marriage to be something different, something rooted in His love and not the whims of human passion.

I love how Tim Keller describes it perfectly:

In sharp contrast with our culture, the Bible teaches that the essence of marriage is a sacrificial commitment to the good of the other. That means that love is more fundamentally action than emotion. But in talking this way, there is a danger of falling into the opposite error that characterized many ancient and traditional societies. It is possible to see marriage as merely a social transaction, a way of doing your duty to family, tribe and society. Traditional societies made the family the ultimate value in life, and so marriage was a mere transaction that helped your family's interest. By contrast, contemporary Western societies make the individual's happiness the ultimate value, and so marriage becomes primarily an experience of romantic fulfillment. But the Bible sees GOD as the supreme good - not the individual or the family - and that gives us a view of marriage that intimately unites feelings AND duty, passion AND promise. That is because at the heart of the Biblical idea of marriage is the covenant.

Reshape how you view marriage, and you will

experience the fullness of what God created marriage for. Dare to be counter-cultural and walk in the purpose that God has created for the marriage that He has led you to. When you do, He will bless your marriage abundantly, and the type of bond that you now enjoy with your spouse will help you to weather the storm of any conflict and come out even stronger on the other side.

Reflection Questions

1. After reading this chapter, what have you learned about God's design for marriage? How does that impact how you see your marriage? How will it change how you live it out?

2. How does understanding God's design for marriage help us to grow in love and patience with our spouse? How does that aid us in conflict resolution in marriage?

Action Tips

➤ Read **Ephesians 5:21-32** together. What do you think that God is trying to speak into your marriage through this passage? Discuss with one another.

➤ Pray with your spouse and ask that God would manifest His design for marriage within your relationship. Ask Him for the wisdom necessary to walk in the fullness of marriage with your spouse.

> ➢ If your spouse fully on-board or aware of God's design for marriage, gently find opportunities to speak together about it. Take it piece by piece, and never push if your spouse isn't ready to go further in the conversation.

Scripture for Prayer and Reflection:

Ecclesiastes 4:9-12: "*Two are better than one, because they have a good reward for their toil. For if they fall, one will lift up his fellow. But woe to him who is alone when he falls and has not another to lift him up! Again, if two lie together, they keep warm, but how can one keep warm alone? And though a man might prevail against one who is alone, two will withstand him—a threefold cord is not quickly broken.*"

Genesis 1:27-28: "*So God created man in his own image, in the image of God he created him; male and female he created them. And God blessed them. And God said to them, "Be fruitful and multiply and fill the earth and subdue it and have dominion over the fish of the sea and over the birds of the heavens and over every living thing that moves on the earth.*"

Prayer

Lord, thank You for Your perfect design for marriage and how it brings us closer to You. Help us to develop understand marriage according to Your design and live it out in ways that please You. We long to honor You through our relationship. Amen.

CHAPTER 10:

Contentment

"Next to faith this is the highest art - to be content with the calling in which God has placed you."

-Martin Luther-

Contentment can be a very challenging state of being to achieve in our modern world. Everything around us pushes so strongly against it. Everywhere we turn we are bombarded with advertisements that attempt to make us feel as if we are missing something. This feeling is encouraged so that we will buy the latest product available in order to fill that particular "gap" in our lives. Not only that, but the media we consume on a daily basis presents bloated and fantastical representations of life that often make us feel as if we are lacking in some way, because our lives don't look like what we see on our TVs.

Contentment is essential to having a healthy marriage. Why? Because if you are not content in life and faith outside of marriage, you won't be inside of marriage either. A marriage thrives when two content people come together and live a mutual life focused on God. Marriage is not meant to be a band-aid that helps heal any pain you are feeling in your life. Can marriage bring you joy? Yes! Can marriage bring fulfillment? Yes! But you have to come to marriage with a content heart rooted in the Lord.

These types of things destroy our feelings of contentment, but we must strive to reclaim it. The truth of the matter is that no matter where we find ourselves in life, we already have everything we need. Paul realized this in his own life, and expressed it in a profound way in **Philippians**

4:10-13: *"I rejoiced greatly in the LORD that at last you renewed your concern for me. Indeed, you were concerned, but you had no opportunity to show it. I am not saying this because I am in need, for I have learned to be content whatever the circumstances. I know what it is to be in need, and I know what it is to have plenty. I have learned the secret of being content in any and every situation, whether well fed or hungry, whether living in plenty or in want. I can do all this through him who gives me strength."*

Paul had gone through many different phases of his life. There were times when he had plenty, and times he was in dire need. But he says he learned to be content in all circumstances. He said that he learned the *secret* to finding contentment despite what was going on around him. What is this powerful and glorious secret? How can we attain it ourselves so that we too can live a life of contentment in all situations?

The secret is that *"I can do all things through Christ who gives me strength."* The secret is that we already have everything we need! There may be things we want, or things that would make our lives easier, but our needs are already met. We have Christ's power within us, and that power can lead us to achieving anything in His name. This power arises from the Holy Spirit within us and is the same immense power that rose Jesus from the dead. It's might has no equal.

This power is manifested in our lives through the meditative practice of prayer. Like I said, contentment is hard, so we must return to prayer daily to reflect on it. It's crucial that we start each day in prayer, thanking God for all that He has given us and for His continual presence within us. This stance of gratitude will help us to always keep in the forefront of our mind the truth that with Jesus in our lives, nothing can hold us back. We are already conquerors through Him.

What is being content? Let's look at some Scriptures to help us better understand the depths of contentment. **Romans 12:12** says, *"Be joyful in hope, patient in affliction, faithful in prayer."* All three things that Paul mentions here relate to cultivating a content heart, but what do they have in common? Consistency. Consistency is something we must pursue and works towards, not something that merely falls into our laps.

So, when Paul says to be joyful in hope, it means that we must continually meditate on hope through prayer. In conversation with God, we are reminded about the reason for our hope: Jesus' sacrificial work on the cross and our promise of eternal life with God. It's crucial that we revisit this hope on a daily basis, and then the joyful spirit will follow.

To be patient in affliction requires similar consistency. It seems as if there is always some kind of trial in life, whether great or small. But if we are cultivating that content spirit within ourselves daily it will help us to persevere and whether the storm more effectively. Times of great trial may require even further deep-diving into our time of reflective, meditative prayer. There, God can remind us of His plans for us, His promise of eternity, and that the things we face here are only temporary. He will help us stand tall in the knowledge that He is for us and that His mighty strength will ultimately prevail over all.

Being faithful in prayer is what building contentment is all about. It is the solid foundation between our feet. Having the safe, consistent, and edifying place of prayer to return to on a daily basis give us the hope, confidence and strength we need to rest in the Lord. That consistency floods our hearts with contentment, because our lives our rooted in God despite what happens in the world around us.

In 1 Timothy, Paul talks of not fixating on material gain or money, however important it is. Contentment simply dwells in uncertainty with hope in God and releases the soul to simply be present with God. Contentment is found in regular prayer with God and meditating on the fact that (**1 Timothy 6:6**) "*we brought nothing into the world and can take nothing out of it.*"

1 Timothy 6:6-7 says, "*But godliness with contentment is great gain. For we brought nothing into the world, and we can take nothing out of* *it.*" It's crucial to remember that the things of this world are only temporary. That's why the forces of evil can take and take from us in this life but will never ultimately defeat us. **Romans 8:11** tells us, "*And if the Spirit of him who raised Jesus from the dead is living in you, he who raised Christ from the dead will also give life to your mortal bodies because of his Spirit who lives in you.*"

This is a remarkable truth. The very same Spirit that made the miraculous miracle of Christ rising from the grave a reality is alive and working with us. That knowledge gives us the reassurance we need to live content lives. The Holy Spirit within us gives us the strength of mind to realize that the battle has already been won and that we are equipped to face anything that comes our way through the power of Christ. We are people with a purpose, mission, and identity in Christ that can not be shaken by even the fiercest storms.

Contentment (and much other godly wisdom) is counter-cultural to the world around us. In **2 Corinthians 12:8-10,** Paul is speaking about a struggle he was going through in life. As he is reflecting on it, he has this to say: "*Three times I pleaded with the Lord to take it away from me. But he said to me, "My grace is sufficient for you, for my power is made perfect in weakness." Therefore I will boast all the more gladly about my weaknesses, so that Christ's power may rest on me. That is why, for Christ's sake, I* *delight in weaknesses, in insults, in hardships, in persecutions, in difficulties. For when I am weak, then I am strong."*

This flipping around of what it means to be strong is what contentment is all about. Our contentment and peace is rattled in this life when our own power fails us and we feel helpless, weak, and without hope. The moment we realize we are not strong enough to handle what's come against us, we begin to lose our contentment. But that's because our conception of what it means to be strong is not accurate.

Strength doesn't lay within ourselves, but within our faith. When we realize that we are weak on our own and require the strength of Christ to persevere, then we are truly strong. It's only then we embody real strength and find contentment, knowing that Jesus has our back always.

But contentment is even more than this. At the end of the day, it is all about simply resting in God's presence. Just as we once felt safe, secure, and content in the arms of our parents when we were children, we too can rest in the presence of our Father today. That's why it's so helpful to look at our relationship with God in the Father/child dynamic.

Recall a memory of a time when you just spent a while talking to your spouse. Likely, all your other troubles had dissipated, your mind free of your responsibilities and trials. You were lost in that moment, not looking at the clock but losing yourself in the time you spent together. You felt contentment in that moment. There was a clarity that is hard to find in life, a place of true rest and renewal.

This is what is possible with God through prayer, but on a whole other level. That's because your relationship with God is the defining relationship of your life and the most special relationship you'll ever have. When you dive deeply into prayer with Him, lose yourself in His presence. Don't worry about the time, anything else you have to do, or other things that have been plaguing your mind. Just focusing on enjoying His presence and conversing with Him.

Be completely present when you are before the Lord. Put your phone away and eliminate as many distractions as possible. When you come to that place before the Lord, you will encounter incredible rest and renewal that your soul needs. Contentment will come as a natural benefit of this. As you feel refreshed in God's presence, His peace and comfort will overwhelm your heart. That peace will mold and reshape your shape into one of contentment. That's because you'll realize very quickly that when you have the Lord's presence in your life, you already have everything you need!

There is a powerful lesson to be learned in Hebrews 13:5-6: *"Don't love money; be satisfied with what you have. For God has said, "I will never fail you. I will never abandon you." So we can say with confidence, "The* LORD *is my helper, so I will have no fear. What can mere people do to me?"* Oftentimes, people's dissatisfaction in life revolves around money. But this is a dangerous cycle, because it seems that no matter how much money people have, they still want more. Many people are never satisfied with money, no matter how much they earn. That's precisely why financial problems are one of the biggest causes of divorce! Married couples tend to argue about money all the time.

That's why the author of Hebrews tells us not to love money. We need money, of course, but what God's Word is trying to tell us is that we should not let it become a desire of our heart. We must use money for its own purposes and leave it at that. We should never long for or covet it. What's interesting about this verse is how the author answers the question of why we shouldn't love money. He says it's because *"The Lord has said, 'I will never fail you. I will never abandon you."*

At first, this answer seems a little strange. What does God's unwavering presence in our lives have to do with money? But upon second look, the author of Hebrews is making a profound point. He is saying that if money has become such a desire of your heart that you've fallen in love with it, your primary focus has shifted from where it needs to be: God. Money has then become an idol in your life. And idols never bring contentment: only more want. True contentment is found in God and God alone, who is always available through prayer.

We must put money in its proper place in our lives so that it doesn't come in the way of our relationship with our spouse or with God!

Bilal Zahoor once said, "Happiness will never come to those who fail to appreciate what they already have." This statement is profound and so true. Everything we have in this life is a stewardship from God. We must be good stewards of the blessings He has provided us with, and if we are not, how can we expect any more?

In Luke 16, Jesus tells a parable about stewardship. Jesus speaks earnestly about the importance of handling the things we are entrusted with to the best of our abilities. He desired to teach the people an important lesson. The story is found in **Luke 16:1-9:**

Jesus told his disciples: "There was a rich man whose manager was accused of wasting his possessions. So he called him in and asked him, 'What is this I hear about you? Give an account of your management, because you cannot be manager any longer.' "The manager said to himself, 'What shall I do now? My master is taking away my job. I'm not strong enough to dig, and I'm ashamed to beg— I know what I'll do so that, when I lose my job here, people will welcome me into their houses.' "So he called in each one of his master's debtors. He asked the first, 'How much do you owe my master?' "'Nine hundred gallons[a] of olive oil,' he replied. "The manager told him, 'Take your bill, sit down quickly, and make it four hundred and fifty.' "Then he asked the second, 'And how much do you owe?' "'A thousand bushels of wheat,' he replied. "He told him, 'Take your bill and make it eight hundred.' "The master commended the dishonest manager because he had acted shrewdly. For the people of this world are more shrewd in dealing with their own kind than are the people of the light. I tell you, use worldly wealth to gain friends for yourselves, so that when it is gone, you will be welcomed into eternal dwellings.

Our lives are all about stewardship when you really think about it. God created the world and everything in it: thus, everything belongs to the Lord. We take nothing with us when we pass from this life. That means that everything we have is on loan from God Himself. He calls us to be faithful stewards of all His blessings. In doing so, we honor Him, we are good witnesses to others, and we don't allow anything we have to become an idol in our lives.

Jesus goes on to drive home his point. In **Luke 16:10-12**, Jesus says, "*whoever can be trusted with very little can also be trusted with much, and whoever is dishonest with very little will also be* *dishonest with much. So if you have not been trustworthy in handling worldly wealth, who will trust you with true riches? And if you have not been trustworthy with someone else's property, who will give you property of your own*?" If we expect to have the best marriage we could possibly have, we must first be content with God. We can't rely on our spouses to bring us ultimate fulfillment in every way. Our hearts must be content in God and God alone, for He is the one who truly satiates our hearts.

James 1:2-4 says, *"Consider it pure joy, my brothers and sisters, whenever you face trials of many kinds, because you know that the testing of your faith produces perseverance. Let perseverance finish its work so that you may be mature and complete, not lacking anything."*

What an interesting verse this is. We are told to count our trials as pure joy. That is something hard to fathom, but as I illustrated in the story, God is able to give us a joy that persists even in the hardest of times. His power is stronger than any hardship we will ever face. He shares His power with us, filling us with joy unending.

We will face trials in life and marriage. It is unavoidable. When we first profess faith in Christ, it doesn't come with the guarantee that God will shield us from the troubles of the world. Many of us come into our faith with some degree of that mindset lingering within us. We are so filled with God's love, peace, and security that we forget how so many have suffered for the faith through the history of Christianity. We are not exempt from this.

The Christian life is not about trying to avoid pain or trials. It's all about how we process and handle these difficulties. The same is true in our marriage. Are we going to take the hurt and pain we experience and let it turn into bitterness? Or are we going to embrace God's love, peace, and joy, instead showing our spouse the unconditional love of God?

Let's explore God's perspective on trials further so we can be everything we can be for our spouses. In the Parable of the Lost Sheep, Jesus tells us an interesting story.

Matthew 18:12-14: *"What do you think? If a man owns a hundred sheep, and one of them wanders away, will he not leave the ninety-nine on the hills and go to look for the one that wandered off? And if he finds it, truly I tell you, he is happier about that one sheep than about the ninety-nine that did not wander off. In the same way, your father in heaven is not willing that any of these little ones should perish."*

This parable reminds us that we continue to suffer the trials of this life because God desires that none are lost. Before the full realization of His coming Kingdom, He has given us the mission to preach the Gospel to the lost so that they would come to salvation. We endure hardships in this life in order to serve those that have not yet come to faith in Christ. Jesus did the same thing! In doing this, we share in His suffering and emulate Him. No matter how hard it may be, we must see it as the honor and privilege that it is.

We can rest assured of our eternal destiny. It is secured in our salvation. The pain of this life is only temporary. The trials that we face in the world grant us the opportunity to grow.

Through prayer, in every trial, ask God to show you what you can learn from the situation. Ask Him for the strength and perseverance to see it through. Find joy in Him, knowing that He will guide you safely to the other side. Cling tightly to His promise of eternity, where you will meet Him face to face, and He will wipe every tear from your eyes. **Romans 8:28** says, *"And we know that in all things god works for the good of those who love Him, who have been called according to His purpose."*

We can trust that God is working behind the scenes to bring us exactly where He wants us to be. We can trust in Him always. His perspective is so much bigger than ours! From our limited human viewpoint, it may seem as if our suffering will never end and that it has no purpose. But just like in the story I told earlier, God has a plan for your life on the other side. All you have to do is put your faith and trust in Him. He will never let you down.

1 Peter 1:6-7 further drives home the joy that is available to us in our pain. Peter writes, "*In all this, you greatly rejoice, though now for a little while you may have had to suffer grief in all kinds of trials. These have come so that the proven genuineness of your faith-of greater worth than gold, which perishes even though refined by fire may result in praise, glory, and honor when Jesus Christ is revealed.*" Peter tells us to "greatly rejoice" in our trials because we have an eternal destiny that cannot be taken from us.

The enemy is real and wants to steal and destroy. He wants to hurt us deeper than we have ever been hurt, but we must not lose hope. Christ has always attained victory over death and evil on the Cross. He has earned our salvation, and now nothing can ever come against us. The brilliant light of Christ's love and sacrifice banishes all of the darkness that we face.

Let's look at one more powerful story, this one from the Bible. King David is described as "a man after God's own heart." He loved the Lord with all His heart. He was human like we are all, and he made mistakes as we all do, but he pursued the Lord with a devotion that we would be wise to imitate.

He wrote a large portion of the Book of Psalms. What's interesting about the Psalms is that 2/3 of the entire book are Psalms of lament! You see,

David went through many trials throughout his life, despite his unwavering devotion to God. David was under constant pressure to defend his people and homeland from the invasion of enemies who would do them harm. He was faithful to King Saul, yet Saul became jealous of David and forced him to live a life on the run in order to save his own life. David's son Amnon committed a grave sin that pained David's heart. His other son Absolom killed Amnon because of that sin and then turned his back on David as well. These unimaginable trials are just a couple on a long list of things that David endured.

But what's remarkable about David is the fact that even in his Psalms of lament, he expresses his trust and hope in the Lord. He even praises God despite what he is going through! His reliance on God brings him past his despair and helps build deep perseverance within him. He knew that God would be faithful to His promises just as He always had been. David's unwavering faith and the endurance that he found in his trust in the Lord should serve as powerful inspiration for us all.

In **John 16:33**, Jesus says, *"I have told you these things, so that in me you may have peace. In this world, you will have trouble. But take heart! I have overcome the world."* Jesus has overcome death on a cross so that you may have victory over your trials. He overcame the enemy and has given you true freedom through Him. You are no longer stuck in the despair that your trials bring to you. You have freedom, power, and joy in Christ that nothing can ever tear away from you.

You are a child of God under His divine protection. You fight battles here in this world for the cause of the Gospel, but you have an eternal home that you will one day return to. The peace and security that you receive from that truth will fuel your joy in this life as you look past your troubles here and into the eternity to come.

Trust in God, embrace your freedom in Christ, and receive the boundless joy that will carry you through everything in life. This is what God desires for you and what is available to you today. If you've not given your life to Christ, there is no better moment than right now. He will give you all of these things when you walk through life with Him. If you are already a believer, recommit yourself to Him, and claim everything that He offers you. Either way, Jesus is waiting for you with open arms. Run to Him, and rest in His embrace. With the transformation you find there, you will be able to be patient, forgiving, and loving in marriage, no matter what trials you may be facing personally or as a couple.

Conclusion

Resolving Conflict God's Way

Let's pull everything we've learned together and recap how to resolve conflict in a godly way.

➢ **Pray Together:** Make sure you have both given your heart, life, and marriage to Christ. Through prayer, God will guide you through your conflict and into newfound growth in your marriage.

➢ **Forgive One Another:** Forgive your spouse, just as God forgave you. Holding grudges never solves anything. It only serves to escalate the conflict. Anger left unresolved will grow and fester until it tears your relationship completely apart.

➢ **Learn to Compromise:** Be flexible and empathetic. Realize that you're not going to get your way all the time, and that's OK! Truly listen to and strive to meet your partner's needs above your own. In doing so, you will be serving them and God.

➢ **Let Emotional Resolve be the Goal:** Step away and cool off when things get heated. Have emotional resolve. Remember that harsh and hurtful words are easy to avoid than to take away. The pain they cause is difficult to heal. It's better never to say those things at all.

➢ **Assume Responsibility:** Resist pride and the tendency to become defensive. Realize that it's not you vs your spouse. You are a team, and you must work through the conflict together. You each have your role to play.

➢ **Stick to the Subject Matter:** Make sure that your discussions revolve around the area of conflict. Throwing other things into the mix that have nothing to do with the matter at hand just escalates the conflict.

➢ **Be Loving, Wise, Gentle, and Honest:** Commit to expressing the fruits of the Spirit in every conversation with your spouse. God has called you to only speak in loving ways to your spouse. There is never an excuse to do things any differently.

➢ **Eliminate the Following Phrases:** You never, you always, I can't, I'll try, you should, or you shouldn't.

➢ **Be a Good Listener:** Truly listen to your spouse's concerns, feelings, wants, and needs. As one flesh in the Lord, your spouse's feelings and concerns should be your own as well.

If you follow these guidelines, you'll not only resolve any conflict that comes your way in marriage, but you will find newfound growth within your marriage. God will bless your efforts to live at peace with one another and bring you into the fullness of what He has designed for your marriage.

Not only that, but He will call you into a glorious purpose as a couple. He can use your marriage to change the world. As man and woman unified under God, you reflect His image more profoundly. Let your marriage shine and become a witness to a world in desperate need of such a witness. In doing so, you will be doing your part in building up the everlasting Kingdom of God.

Living Out the Call to Love

When you think of marriage, it's likely the first thing you think of is love. That makes sense because feelings of attraction, admiration, and love are what initially draw us to our spouses. These feelings are very strong at the beginning of our relationships and a huge motivation as begin a lifelong journey together.

What we must realize is that love is a much broader and deeper word than we have come to understand it. Take all of your preconceived notions of what love is based on what you see on TV or in the movies and throw it in the trash. That is not real, genuine love. Love is about SO MUCH MORE!

Love is such a deep and powerful word that there are four different words used for it in the Greek

New Testament, its original language. They each carry a particular meaning with them. This very truth makes evident the unbelievable depth of this emotion and its importance in God's story. The first word used for love in the New Testament is στοργ (*storge*). This word refers to the love we have for our family, whether it be our parents, siblings, children, or any other family member. This is the word used for "love" in Romans 1:31 when Paul writes about pagans: "*They have no understanding, no fidelity, no love, no mercy.*"

Another word used for love is φιλία (*philia*). This word can best be described as "brotherly love." It is the type of affection that you carry for your close friends. It is the word that is used to describe Jesus' love for His disciple in John 20:2: "*So she came running to Simon Peter and the other disciple, the one Jesus loved, and said, "They have taken the LORD out of the tomb, and we don't know where they have put him!*"

There is also Ερως (*eros*). *Eros* is sexual, intimate love. It is an interesting word because it goes much deeper than this. *Eros* carries with it an appreciation and love for the beauty within another person. It's a beautiful way to think of intimate, erotic love with your spouse. Your desire to connect with them physically is the result of your deep love and appreciation for the beauty that you see within them. These two things are inseparably linked. The physical act of sex because more than a physical experience. It becomes an act where the couple connects body, mind, and soul.

Another beautiful, profound word for love in the New Testament is ἀγάπη (*agape*). This world describes the all-encompassing love that God has for humanity and creation itself. This is also the kind of love that Jesus calls us to have for everyone, even our enemies. *Agape* love is the most powerful form of love, knowing no boundaries, no limits, no equal in strength, and no end. *Agape* love is the divine love of God from which we were created. It is the kind of love that turns hearts of stone back into hearts of flesh. This form of love is the love that through Jesus Christ brings everyone who accepts it the free gift of eternal life with God in His fully realized Kingdom.

Now, all of these types of love are important to our marriage. Each depth of meaning in the word love speaks to an aspect of our relationship. For instance, our partner is not only our spouse (or soon-to-be-spouse) but also our friend. The kind of affection we feel for our friends should be prevalent in our relationship. This is *philia*.

Then, there is *storge*, familial love. Not only is our partner our friend, but when we marry, they also become family. So, *storge* love should resonate within our hearts for our partners as well! *Agape* love is also crucial to our marriages. The love between us and our partners should be built on the foundation of the *agape* love in which

God loves us. God's love for us individually and as a couple should define our relationship.

Eros is self-explanatory but wildly important. This love is unique because it's *only* for our spouse. While each and every other kind of love is appropriate for other relationships, God created *eros* for the sole purpose of being expressed by husband and wife. This love is important to be cherished, protected, and celebrated through every step of your marriage. It's crucial that you always fan the flames of *eros* love and share that beautiful intimacy with your partner.

Through this word study, we see that love is so much more and profoundly deeper than what the world portrays it as. As we meditate on love through prayer, we must keep in mind the scope of God's perspective on love rather than based our thoughts on our own limited human perspective. We must strive towards the love that we experience in the Bible, not the over dramatized versions we see on the big screen. This is the key to experiencing lasting love throughout your entire marriage and not the kind that fades as we get older like we see in so many other couples.

Remember, God's Word tells us that God *is* love. God's very nature and character define what love is. Are we to believe that God's character is as small as a human understanding of love? Absolutely not. If God is love, that means that love is as vast, mysterious, beautiful, and endless as God's character.

As you meditate on love through prayer, consider what happens when this kind of love enters your heart. Imagine how our capacity for love expands, how our vision for our lives branches out, and how our view of our world changes. This is how we are drawn toward seeking out the will of God instead of our own. Ask God to help you experience this remarkable transformation.

When asked what the greatest commandment in all the Scriptures was, Jesus expressed the irreplaceable position of love. We find this story in **Matthew 22:36-40**: *"Teacher, which is the greatest commandment in the Law?"* Jesus replied: *"'Love the Lord your God with all your heart and with all your soul and with all your mind.' This is the first and greatest commandment. And the second is like it: 'Love your neighbor as yourself.' All the Law and the Prophets hang on these two commandments."*

Notice that both of these two commandments focus on love: love for God, love for ourselves, and love for others. Not only that, but Jesus says that the entirety of the Scriptures hang on these two commandments! So, what He is trying to tell us is that love is the embodiment of all that is important to God. It must define the way we live. That's why it's essential to meditate on love through prayer. Prayer can help us become people that love fiercely and unconditionally, just like the Lord we serve. This kind of love is the love we must love our spouse with.

1 John 4:9 says, *"We love because He first loved us."* God's love perpetuates the unconditional advance of love. All we must do to be a part of this movement of love is to step within its flow daily through prayer and carry it with us throughout the remainder of our day. When we do, God's love will radiate from us, transforming our relationship and our lives in remarkable ways.

Reflection Questions

1. How is God's definition and design for love different than that of the world around us?

2. How are the four different Greek words for love helpful for our understanding of what love in marriage is all about?

Action Points

➢ Discuss the four types of love with your partner. Take turns coming up with examples of each in your life and in your relationship.

➢ Have a conversation with your spouse about how godly love differs from what we see in the movies. Make a list comparing and contrasting the two. Make goals for how you can better exemplify godly love through your relationship.

Scripture for Prayer and Reflection

Matthew 22:36-40: *"Teacher, which is the greatest commandment in the Law?"* Jesus replied: *"'Love the Lord your God with all your heart and with all your soul and with all your mind.' This is the first and greatest commandment. And the second is like it: 'Love your neighbor as yourself.' All the Law and the Prophets hang on these two commandments."*

1 John 4:9: *"We love because He first loved us."*

Prayer

Lord, thank You for the joy of love. We are grateful for the way it reflects You, draws us closer to You, and enriches our lives. Help us to celebrate and grow in our love daily. Let us love one another in a way that draws us ever closer to you. Amen.

In Closing: Going the Distance

If you want your marriage to go the distance, you're going to have to perform regular maintenance. A healthy, thriving, and life-giving marriage doesn't happen by itself: you've got to put the work in!

Together, we have discussed the mechanics of marriage. Like a car, you have to perform regular tune-ups on all aspects of your marriage to keep it in tip-top shape. Letting even one area of your marriage slip into disrepair can have disastrous effects down the road. No matter how hard it is, it's best to put in the work at the appropriate time so your marriage is finely tuned at all times.

We pray that the wisdom we have unearthed together will help lead you to a marriage abounding in peace, love, and joy. Cling to one another, and more importantly, cling to the Lord. Work through the hard times, celebrate the good ones, and love one another fiercely. Dedicate yourselves to God and walk the path He has paved before you.

Commit to finding balance in your relationship, resolving conflict lovingly, and communicating openly. Even when things get tough, stay in the struggle: what you receive on the other side will be more than worth it. The joy and love that you receive from the effort you put in will far outweigh the hard times it took to get there. Those few moments of tension will result in a lifelong love which will transform both of your lives.

Together, in union with one another and with God, you CAN go the distance! Apply the mechanics of marriage to your relationship and experience all that a godly marriage has to offer.

Made in the USA
Columbia, SC
06 February 2023

11434422R00085